YOUR FIRST GOVERNMENT CONTRACT

CAPTURE AND PROPOSAL WRITING

SCOTT JOHNSON, MBA, PMP

DEDICATION

My wife, Silvia, has been a stable base of support and patience during many proposal-writing "all-nighters" before due dates.

CONTENTS

PART II
SELLING TO THE GOVERNMENT

PART III
**BUILDING A PUBLIC SECTOR
BUSINESS STRATEGY**

PART IV
PLANNING TO WIN

PART V
PROPOSAL PLANNING AND WRITING

PART VI
WHEN THINGS GO RIGHT

PART VII
WRAPPING UP

INTRODUCTION

I don't think people graduate from college or leave the armed forces with a dream of starting a career in government contracting. I only say that because every person I have met in this industry was "doing something else" when they fell into the public sector market.

Government sales are very different from selling to businesses or selling to consumers. Primarily, there isn't any door-knocking or cold calling. Sure, you can do that, but the return on investment for the time and effort won't be good.

Selling to the government is a longer cycle; it is more strategic and technical and takes patience. For those that get good at it, the excitement of the pursuit and win of a great government contract is an exhilaration that selling widgets doesn't provide. If you are selling law enforcement equipment, would you prefer to sell 25 flashlights to a local private security firm or 25,000 of them to a federal law enforcement agency? Negotiating the transaction with a federal contracting officer may take longer, but it's not 1000 times longer. If you are leasing office space, do you want to lease a 1200-square-foot retail storefront suite to the local coffee shop startup for a year, or the whole 250,000-square-foot building to a state government agency for the next 25 years?

This book introduces the public procurement process, a basic understanding of public sector marketing "do's" and "don't," how to locate and appraise opportunities, and a strategy for designing and writing a winning proposal in response.

PART I

GETTING STARTED

1

NAPKIN MATH

Everyone has heard the [factual] statement that the US federal government is the world's largest customer. It deserves to be well-known since it's true. Rather than repeat the same cliches, I have provided some researched facts.

Using what I call "napkin math," a term I will often use throughout this book. I have a natural gift for estimation and doing so instantly. If I am in a store looking at a product for $100, and the local tax rate is 7.375%, in a quarter of a second, I know the cost out of pocket will be about $107.38. Suppose it is a capitalized business purchase with a more extended depreciation schedule, like office furniture. In that case, I'll also calculate about $1 in net federal income tax obligation (15% federal corporate tax minus 1/7 of the $100 for first-year depreciation), a $15 tax obligation minus about $14 of depreciation. Are the actual numbers going to calculate differently? Yes, probably, but in 2 seconds, I have enough information to decide. I am talking about this because it is a critical skill in government contracting. We do not always have the luxury of working with perfect information or the time we need to decide. Sometimes we have to go with what we have.

We can reach small-dollar and large-margin decisions quickly this way. When the downside risk is insignificant, a small amount of money, the business risk is negligible. When the product or service margins are always high, decisions are also easier to make.

The napkin math method is not as effective for the middle ground when tight margins or a large amount of money is involved. More care is needed, and more is taken.

The danger in public sector contracting is the opposite when people spend so much time researching that they develop what I would call "analysis paralysis." Analysis paralysis is spending so much time trying to decide that the labor cost of the analysis exceeds the profit potential - or the inability to reach a decision, no matter how much information is obtained. Unable to make decisions to move forward or abandon the opportunity compounds into a very high opportunity cost. It is certainly common in government, and I think it sometimes spills over into the contracting sector.

In 2021, the gross domestic product (GDP) of the United States was about $24.8 trillion. In the same year, the US Government committed to $1.1 trillion of contractual obligations for goods and services for about 4% of the US economy); this figure does not include non-discretionary spending, such as Medicare and Medicaid, or defense. In other words, about $1 out of every $20 spent in the US was paid by the US [federal] government [taxpayers] to buy stuff (separate from government salaries and programs).

According to the System of Award Management (Sam.gov), the top 100 US government contractors received $262,136,056,000 ($262.1 billion) of new contract awards in 2021, or about $2.621 billion each. We have about 8 million businesses in the US, but only 802,000 are registered entities on Sam.gov, an absolute minimum requirement to receive any money from the federal government. About 100,000 of those are other public sector agencies, departments, organizations, states, cities, and counties receiving federal funds transfers. So about 700,000 businesses out of the 8 million split $837.9 billion of spending. 700,000 is a lot of competitors, but it is also a lot of money and averages \$1.197 million per business. Is it profitable? It can be. 0.00125% of the companies in the US (100 out of 8 million[1]) are taking in 1.057% of the economy (\$262.1 billion out of \$24.8 trillion). Considered another way, they are over-performing their GDP "share" by about 73,990x.

It is Much Larger

The citable government statistics focus on only the federal government, or only [each] state government. It is much more significant if the estimates of government spending aggregate the federal, state, and local governments, utility districts, universities, public schools, armed forces, national guard, public health care, Social Security, public pension funds, and others. I have seen estimates as high as 38% to 41% of the US GDP. As an educated guess, I think it is closer to 25%.

A large portion of this cost is transferred to individuals through salaries, pensions, or Social Security benefits and spent on consumer stuff. But I think a safe bet is a state and local governments spend at least as much in aggregate as the federal government on private contractors, so whatever federal government estimates of contractor spending are out there, we assume the state and local aggregate is at least as significant.

What is the Lesson?

I bring these researched statistics up for two reasons. First, I have skimmed through several "selling stuff to the government books" that seem to have been written by people that have never sold anything to the government. Instead, they focus on how to "get registered" or how to post your stuff on an e-procurement website. I even previewed one that was a step-by-step on how to get an employer ID number and open a bank account. I suppose there is value in that, but frankly, not much, and I would put the odds of success for those approaches at about 0.1%. They may get lucky, or there might be a brother-in-law that is the city engineer in charge of public works procurements, but in a straight-up competition, it will take much more than the bare minimum to be successful.

Comparing Three Contractors

If you were going to build a house to spend your retirement in and invest much of your life's savings in it, you would probably request several bids unless your brother-in-law is a contractor, and you don't want things to be awkward at Thanksgiving.

The first offer comes in, and it is wildly extravagant. You asked for a 2500 square foot single-story house on a modest lot that you own, and you are looking at blueprints for a 3-story cliffhanger with decks on each floor overlooking an ocean view with 6,000 square feet of living space. It may be fantastic, but it's out of your price range. Could you come up with the money? Maybe, but you probably don't want another mortgage payment when entering your retirement.

Offer two has been received and is close to what you want. The contractor presenting it has been building similar houses for twenty years, has a crew available, and has robust relationships with local subcontractors and material suppliers. The budget is reasonable and in line with your target.

Offer three comes in, and it is half of your budget estimation, it sort of looks like what you want, but the contractor just got his or her license yesterday. The offer does not include a performance bond, and it is doubtful that the new contractor has a workers' compensation policy. Your project is the first offer the new contractor has ever submitted, and until last week was working as a plumber's apprentice for six months for one of the subs listed on offer #2.

Which one would you choose? You can't afford offer #1, offer #3 looks very risky, and you feel you could quickly end up with little more than a pile of discarded lumber left on your building lot when they fold up and run away, and #2 is within your budget, exactly what you asked for, and carries a low risk of project failure.

Unless you unexpectedly won the lottery the night before, you will pick #2.

Let's start your plan to be "Contractor #2."

---

1. IBISWorld. (2022). https://www.ibisworld.com/us/bed/number-of-businesses/2898/.

2

IS THIS FOR YOU?

The General Services Administration's (GSA) various government-wide acquisition contracts (GWACs) and Federal Supply Schedule (FSS) solicitations have several paragraphs in the introductory section of the solicitation with a paraphrasing of the basic question "Is this for you?"

The GSA's point of the generalized question is a valid one and should be a concern for anyone reading this book. I do not intend to repeat their various ways of asking the same thing and would refer you to use their online vendor training materials. Instead, I want to focus on these three questions:

1. Is your company ready for this?
2. Is the government interested in your products or services?
3. Can your company be competitive in the government contracting market?

Unfortunately, only about 10% of the contractors that obtain a GSA GWAC or FSS award will ever successfully sell something using those types of contracts. There are many reasons for this, and I will cover some of them later in this chapter. The effort and cost of preparing to enter the government market can be significant, and I recommend you review the remainder of this section and critically analyze your situation before committing your company.

For the remaining 90% of the companies that hold a contract award, even a $1 million sale (out of a $3 billion contracting vehicle) can be a game-changer. Don't let the "90% goes to 10% of contract holders" be a statistic that dissuades you. The average American small business does not have the overhead of a principal government contractor, and a small award will positively impact its future.

Why are So Many Unsuccessful?

There are many reasons why some companies fail, and others will wildly succeed, but I have seen several common and recurring problems. Some of these might be avoidable for you; some may not be, so let's be frank and calculate the cost and the risk.

Sales Capacity

Selling to the government takes patience, quality, and the value of the messaging to the agency. It would be best if you also had consistency, networking, and the ability to identify and reach decision-makers and influencers.

Small business owners will often underestimate the sales capabilities of their larger competitors. There may not be a difference between the product quality of a Fortune 500 company versus a family-owned manufacturing firm, but there is a vast difference in the size of the sales teams. When representing medium-sized firms, I have built teaming partnerships between a supplying firm and a more significant Fortune 500 or 1000 partner where the entire headcount of the medium-sized company is smaller than just the state & local sales team for one business unit of the multi-national.

Why does this matter? There are strengths and vulnerabilities for each.

The Small to Medium Entrepreneur

An entrepreneur considering a public sector sales division may already be regarded as a very successful individual. There is confidence in their available resources to lay out the cost to do so in advance and understand the risk may be getting nothing in return. Entrepreneurs attempting to do so should be "scrappy" concerning their tenacity but not "crappy" about their product or service quality. To get that chance at a broader future for your company, you need to strive to be the best at what you do.

The smaller firm's strengths are:

1. The ability to make a decision rapidly
2. Pricing flexibility
3. And the ability to quickly pivot and reprioritize to take on a new contract award or product supply request from their partner

Another strength of a smaller firm is patience. The firm can continue to make modest investments of time and resources within a safe budget for future public sector sales goals, and there will not be a lot of pressure from stakeholders to show a return immediately. There may be other family members with financial interests or other shareholders, but as long as the tightly held company's ownership is in agreement on the goals, the patience for the length of time needed for a public sector sales and growth cycle will usually be there.

The vulnerabilities can be short-sightedness and occasionally a level of arrogance. Entrepreneurs have social circles like themselves and are usually very regional or closed within their specific area, expertise, or industry. Their peers may not be in public sector markets either, so their view of the world can be confined to the opinions of their social circle. It is also rare that the business owner has ever worked for a large firm before; it takes years to build their own company, and to do so would not have afforded the time for a 9-5 every day in a cubicle. If you asked someone to build a Ferrari, but they didn't know what it was, had never seen one before, and didn't provide specifications or photos, do you think you would get something that looks like a Ferrari? I don't think so. The same problem exists for an entrepreneur trying to build a sales team that can genuinely compete with one fielded by a large company.

Personalities aside, a smaller firm's most significant disadvantage will be a lack of resources. At some point, the costs incurred need to produce a return, or the firm will need to move on to something that works better and turns a profit. The business owner needs to ask themselves if they are better off expanding what they already do well or making the investments required to expand into the public sector. I can't answer that, but hopefully, some of the information in this book will assist the business owner in making the best choice for their situation.

The Large Firm

Large firms have a different set of advantages and problems. First, they can afford to hire the best expertise they can find, but this also comes at a price and an opportunity cost. At some point, usually every quarter, they are accountable to their shareholders for the investment being made. The resources may be nearly bottomless, but the patience is not. In the public sector, "Time" and "Patience" are more important than "gee-whiz" marketing flashiness. Most requests for proposals (RFPs) will expressly state that submissions should be modestly produced, easy to read, and not indulge in [paraphrasing] "marketing fluff."

The one thing a large firm can do is what I would describe as a "focused agency specialization," for lack of a better description. There may be a buzzword for this, but I don't know it. A handicap of small or medium-sized firms is a lack of sales reach. For example, a small or medium-sized firm may have one or a handful of marketing, business development, and sales professionals focused on public sector sales, versus a large firm will often have several vertical market specialists for each agency or region they are targeting. The specialization and dedication of time and resources can generate much more opportunity intelligence for each upcoming solicitation, making it very difficult for a smaller competitor to prevail in a procurement competition.

The Achilles heel of a large company is often a lower level of customer service, and it can be a profound vulnerability in the public sector market. Agency bureaucracies [rightfully] see themselves as huge customers deserving of the best level of service and at the lowest cost. Smaller firms will usually have an owner directly or closely involved, and the entrepreneurial instinct will be to do whatever it takes to make the customer happy. Account teams for large companies are considerably further removed from that instinct.

It is crucial for aspiring small business government contractors to know and understand the competition.

The Condition of Your Business

The question is one of time and resources. Do you have the time to devote to this effort? Businesses can outsource government marketing to a vendor, but the quality of the output from a consultant will only be as good as your information. The quality of your product or service and the quality of the customer references. Only you know your business, and only you can put your best foot forward. Once the sales pitch is in place, others can help you move the ball forward.

Public Sector Sales and Marketing Plan

The time and effort for putting together the first opportunity sales and proposal plans will be more than you expect the first time you take on a public sector solicitation response.

Outsourcing your first proposal effort can be relatively inexpensive, considering you are buying a significant portion of an educated person's time, but even those approaches are not without a substantial level of effort. Public sector opportunities are a more complex sales process than a business-to-business (B2B) sales effort, so your existing sales materials and approach will probably require some modifications. For example, a business may rarely (or never) mention its past performance or document its customer references for a B2B or B2C sales quote. In contrast, past performance references can be as much as 35% of a public sector proposal evaluation's scoring (or more).

The safe bet would be to budget about 3x-5x the time and resources you typically use for your existing business sales for the first public sector attempt. Remember, this is only an estimate for a generic and straightforward professional services proposal or a narrow product offering. If you are a sole-source provider of your product or service, provide a new product with no other similar offers in the market-place, or have an extensive library of product SKUs, the first effort will be more complex.

You may submit other bids and proposals before the first ones are evaluated and awarded. Even if you win your first bid, several months may transpire before notification of the award is received, and it can be another 30 days (or longer) before you begin performing on the contract. If you are perfect with your proposal, perfect with your pricing, excellent with your past performance, and you are awarded the contract, assume several months from start to finish for the procurement cycle on a small to medium procurement. Ordinary commodity and supplies purchases can be very straightforward, but significant government contracts can take years to plan, solicit, evaluate, and award. Whatever your product and service, be prepared for a little more difficult sales process at first, and you will probably lose more often than you win early in your public sector efforts.

Despite the struggle, you will eventually win your first and second contracts, and this is part of what is considered in the up-front cost I mentioned. You may lose a dozen or more opportunities before winning one. Even if you can perform a vast project, I recommend starting "small" and working your way up if you want some success. Losing too many of these efforts will cost time, resources, travel costs in some cases, and other lost opportunity costs from diverting time and resources away from other potential customers. You will eventually succeed by putting the right team together, analyzing your losses and the reasons for them, and improving your pitch each time. It can take time.

3

BUSINESS STRUCTURES AND HOW YOU IDENTIFY

There are legal, tax, and strategic issues that can determine the best type of business structure for your operation, and your attorney or CPA can provide the best advice for your individual situation. What we should discuss in this book is how your business is identified by the government, and some concerns with how you choose to do so. Unlike the commercial business world, everything you provide to the government is technically a matter of public record.

Tax Identification Numbers

If operating as a sole proprietorship, you can do business with your Social Security Number (SSN), but your SSN will be on many (hundreds or thousands) of documents over time, and will often be found in the public domain. To avoid this and still get started doing business in the public sector, you will want to obtain an Employer Identification Number (EIN) if you do not already have one. Changing this is very painful to do later, particularly if you have contracts underway, so get a permanent solution in place before you get started. You can obtain an EIN quickly on the IRS website.

The US federal government previously required a Dun & Bradstreet (D&B) number and rating, but that requirement quietly went away early in 2022. State and local governments may still need one. If so, assuming your business is actively operating, you probably have a D&B number. D&B scoops up new business registrations, fictitious business name filings, and other business public records and creates a generic reference to your business in their database via automation. For a small, closely held company without any debt, the D&B report may be empty or completely inaccurate in many cases.

A common misconception is that you need to "buy" a D&B report to get more reporting accuracy. In recent years, the government has marginalized the requirement, and contracting officers are accustomed to seeing strange-looking reports for small companies. If selling widgets or professional services, I don't think it is an important consideration. If you are bidding on public works projects with construction bonding, there will be many reasons to correct your D&B report. Call the number on their website and expect it will cost you something to initiate their research.

Sam.gov

Before submitting an offer for a federal solicitation, you must be registered on Sam.gov. Generally, it is good practice to do so before beginning your first offer for any public sector solicitation, including state or local government ones, because many other public sector systems will reference your Sam.gov record. Doing so may avoid unexpected problems elsewhere. After your submission, Sam.gov will automatically compare your submitted profile information to the Internal Revenue Service (IRS) and will automatically assign a NATO CAGE code (Commercial and Government Entity) if you do not already have one. Without a better description, the CAGE code is a license plate for your business and is unique across all of the NATO-allied countries. That is all it is. State and local government procurements may request your offer cover letters, including your CAGE code identifier.

Why is Sam.gov So Important?

SAM is the System for Award Management. While it seems like we may be getting ahead of ourselves, registering in the "award" management system before submitting an offer for anything, registration in Sam.gov is a prerequisite for nearly every other "first" step.

Sam.gov also serves as an excellent quality-control check. If there is a problem with your company formation, banking, or tax status, the issues will be identified during the Sam.gov registration process, and you can correct them before becoming a significant problem delaying your first contract award.

Setting Up Your Sam.gov Profile

Setting up the Sam.gov profile is not something for most "employees" of a company to do themselves without a specific delegation. The owner or a senior officer of the company needs to be directly involved or do this part themselves. Nonetheless, here is the general outline of the steps required.

First, create a login ID for yourself at <u>Sam.gov</u>. Moving a business's <u>Sam.gov</u> record from one registration login ID to another is complicated, so the login ID needs to belong to someone that will be with the company forever - the business owner, CEO, trusted consultant or vendor, etc. The person should be the point of contact for all things contracting for the federal government and your business, and changing it is going to be like trying to get someone at the DMV or the IRS on the phone. It is easier to do this correctly now and avoid losing 20 hours of your life later that you will never get back.

To finish the second step, you will need some information that you may not always have readily available. Have your entity registration information handy, such as the filing certificate for your articles of incorporation or similar for your business entity type, your routing and account numbers for your accounts receivable bank account, and the contact information for critical individuals for your company. Other points of contact to list may include the CEO, sales contacts, accounting, and the individual with knowledge of your past performance (customer references). Hint: updating the contacts for your business entity registration in Sam.gov is easy to do, but you can also set up "group" email addresses - such as "accounting@yourcompany.com," "governmentsales@yourcompany.com," and others. Sam.gov allows group email addresses; this approach also provides copies of important emails to all of the group members. Sam.gov allows the same one or few people to be the same or a limited number of individuals in all of the roles.

Sam.gov Affirmations

Affirmations are statements to which you will read and affirm or disclose an answer accordingly. These are a mixture of what can be thought of as retail politics and socioeconomic information. For example, statements to confirm that you do not do business with the governments of Iran or Sudan and that you comply with prohibitions of trade with Russia and other clauses relevant to the nightly news. It will be elementary for most US companies to affirm their compliance with the regulations. Some are more of a mystery, such as statements regarding "covered telecommunications equipment." When you don't know, enter the phrase or US code paragraph number in your favorite search engine, and you will easily find an explanation.

For the "covered telecommunications equipment" example, the regulation refers to electronics such as 5G cellular network components manufactured by sanctioned Chinese firms, such as Huawei. Since this would be incredibly hard to obtain in the US, you are probably already in compliance. If you own and operate a cellular service carrier in Europe, you may need to research your answer more closely, but for most of us, easy to answer.

Anyone can research the more obscure statements; copy & paste the US Code reference number into a search engine window, and you will probably get the complete draft of the law or regulation. Just review the text. I'm sure some will suggest an attorney do so, and I collaborate with attorneys frequently on a range of public sector contracting issues, but this is one area that I haven't seen a lot of enthusiasm for on their part, and you will be doing this very often for your public sector business operations. Learning the skills yourself sooner rather than later is advised. If you are unsure about one or more, ask a friend (or your attorney). You can permanently save your position and return to your Sam.gov registration later.

Important Sam.gov Considerations

There are a few essential things to get right in your Sam.gov profile. You can always change these later, but they are critical, and I'll summarize them.

Your NAICS code is what the federal government perceives your business as able to offer to them. You can have several if you have multiple lines of business, but your primary should be the #1 thing you want to provide to the federal government. If you subscribe to a solicitation research service, which I will discuss later, you can search for opportunities by the NAICS code assigned to it or from a range of anticipated NAICS codes, such as within a "sources sought" advertisement.

After the Sam.gov interview is completed, the system will spawn the CAGE code request I mentioned earlier and will also verify your company name and tax identification number with the IRS. The IRS verification takes 48 hours, but the CAGE code assignment from the Department of Defense is longer and seems to have humans involved. It states up to ten business days, but I have seen it take around five weeks on one occasion. Don't postpone your initial registration until you have something to bid on; you may not complete the registration in time.

Previously, companies were also required to mail a notarized letter to the Sam.gov help desk certifying business control to the procedure. The requirement was in response to a wave of hack attempts on business profiles. GSA provided a letter template on the Sam.gov website, as well as the instructions for doing so. I haven't seen the requirement in the last few years, but I already have a person/identity established. It may only affect new Sam.gov users, or it may no longer be required. If needed, pick the appropriate one for your business type. My previous experiences with this have taken as long as two or three months. This requirement was forced upon all federal contractors for the first time in 2017, creating a "rush" of new and existing contractors. I expect the process and turnaround times have improved as volume decreased and the internal workflow at the help desk improved. Hopefully, something in-line with the CAGE code turnaround time will develop, but I don't have any recent experience to form an opinion.

Once these steps are complete, you will receive an email stating that your Sam.gov account is activated. You are now ready to bid on posted business opportunities.

Small Businesses

If you are a small business defined for your NAICS code in Sam.gov, you should complete the SBA profile extension within Sam.gov. After doing so, you can bid on compatible small business set-asides for the same NAICS code. Anyone can bid on full & open opportunities at any time, but there are advantages for operating as a small business, and we will discuss them in later chapters.

Several NAICS codes can be considered a fit for your primary type of business. As a tip, if multiple NAICS codes are applicable and your company exceeds the small business limits for some but is considered a small business for others, I suggest using the best-fitting small business option for your primary and adding the others as secondaries. Be sure to explore the thresholds for all potential NAICS codes to use as your primary, but don't consider something too far removed from what you do for a living, or you won't be successful bidding on the opportunities anyway.

You can also bid on any opportunities with NAICS codes listed within your "secondary" NAICS codes in your profile, and you can change these later, add some, move them around, or delete them.

Pro Tip: Sam.gov registrations can inexplicably take longer than anticipated sometimes, be sure to finish this well in advance of your first federal contracting proposal.

Wrapping Up Sam.gov

The rest of your Sam.gov registration is going to be self-explanatory. Identify any problems, correct them, and finish your Sam.gov registration before you submit your first proposal. Keep in mind that minor issues can create a snag that can take a while to resolve, so doing this and knowing it has been completed is a crucial first step.

What if There is No Intention to Compete for Federal Government Business?

This is a great question and one that I would anticipate anyone asking if this is their intention. My answer is Sam.gov is very good at identifying any problems with your business records. If something fails with the Sam.gov registration, it will probably fail everywhere else. Likewise, if Sam.gov accepts your input, you are good to go.

State and Local Procurement Registrations

Registering your business within the state and local e-procurement systems is usually more manageable than the federal government's sam.gov platform. There is one caveat, in my experience, most of the small government procurement systems are a little clunky to use, but they have been improving. There, I said it. It's what I think, and I speak my mind. Plan your time accordingly. I think I have accounts on 45'ish state-level systems and probably two or three dozen accounts on large city and county procurement systems. I see some slick procurement systems from time to time at state & local government levels, but it seems rare.

Password Generators

Usually, online registration for a government procurement system of reasonable quality will take less than ten minutes to finish. Still, you need a separate registration for every state, city, county, school district, utility district, and university you may be interested in pursuing. The need for secure password generation and storage is where an app-based password keeper/database comes in handy. Do not use simple passwords, only the app's complex ones, and never use the same ones twice. Remember, the registration profiles in these systems have tax data, many have banking account records like Sam.gov, and all have the potential to divert a contract payment elsewhere by hijacking your profile. Use a quality password database app.

Pay to Play

State and local registrations are usually straightforward, requiring only your business name, address, EIN, D&B number, website, and personal contact information. For cities and counties, after completing this, you are usually ready to proceed with looking for opportunities.

Some states and local entities have "pay walls" in place, requiring you to submit a fee of some sort, usually annually, before activating your profile. It is how they recover the cost of their public-facing solicitation system. Usually, this will be around $25 to $75, depending on your business type and the state, city, or county.

Depending on your line of work, a bid bond may be customary. I have also seen bid bonds required, like selling off-the-shelf software, when not typical for the industry. I recommend considering your odds of prevailing, how often you will submit a proposal for the given jurisdiction, and other factors when deciding whether or not to submit an offer with registration fees and bonding requirements. The Bid vs. No-Bid decision is a critical part of public sector contracting, and we will discuss this in greater detail in Chapter 5, Bid or No-Bid.

Pro Tip: You will quickly accumulate many login IDs and passwords, with long minimum lengths and complexity standards. A password application with a random password generator feature is highly recommended.

The Capabilities Statement

New participants in the government contracting market may be caught off guard when asked for their "capabilities statement." The statement is unique to the public sector and is probably seldom heard of, if ever, in B2B or B2C sectors.

When you begin to make your first marketing contacts in the public sector market, one of the first two or three will probably ask you for this document. The capabilities statement should be a one-pager with a designed marketing flyer layout; it is your firm's resume, for lack of a better word.

At a minimum, it should always include your Sam.gov Unique Identifier, Dun & Bradstreet number, CAGE code, NAICS codes, socioeconomic designation, and a list of your cooperative contract awards.

If you have sociodemographic certifications, like a Service-Disabled Veteran-Owned Small Business (SDVOSB) or a woman-owned small business, indicate so with the other business identifiers.

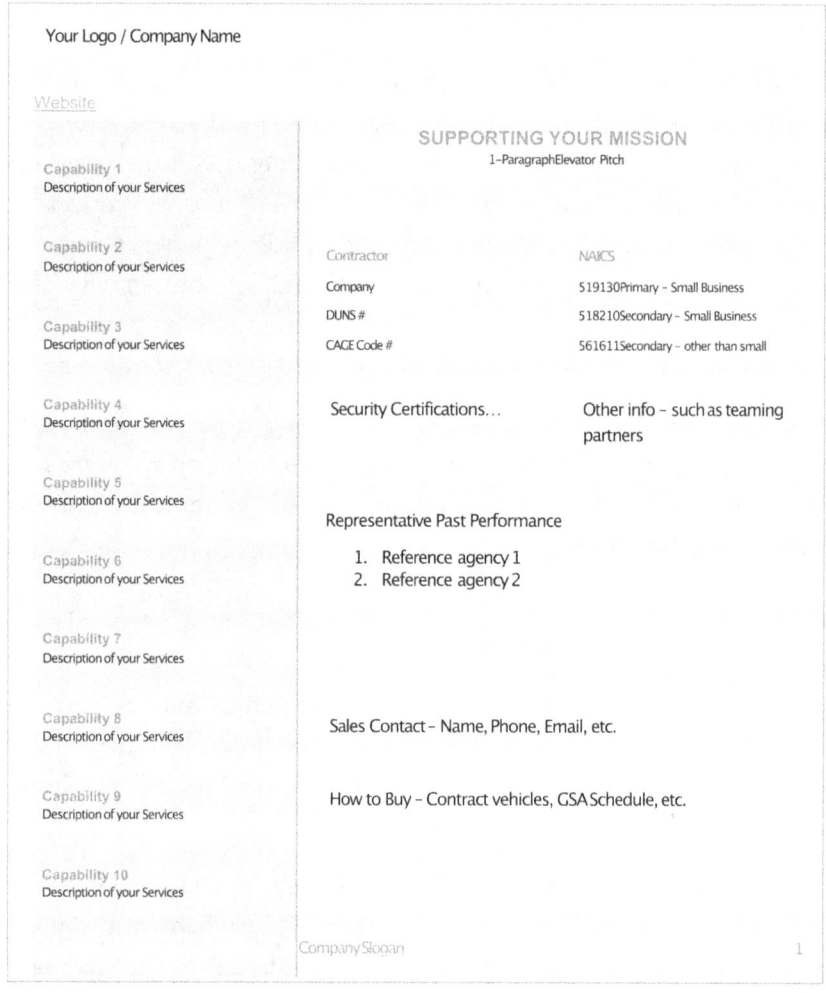

Basic Sample of a Capabilities Statement

Certain socioeconomic groups, such as a HubZone or 8(a) disadvantaged business certification, can obtain a direct award of the opportunity without formal solicitation or competition, so of course, this should be prominently displaced with the authorized logos and certification numbers.

The 15-Second Pitch

I recommend the capabilities statement include a synopsis of what your business can do in an elevator 15-second pitch format, a list of previous government contracts (or commercial if nothing else), any government procurement vehicles you hold, such as GSA schedules, and most importantly, the government agencies where you have recently provided products or services.

Larger prime contracting firms, such as name-your-defense-contractors, will use the capabilities statements to configure your profile within their subcontracting database. Many larger contracts (and even smaller ones) have specific sociodemographic set-asides and require a subcontracting plan to be submitted with the proposal; often, there are designated targets to be reached.

As a habit, I send the capabilities statement to nearly every new contact. It has everything the government agency or prospective teaming partner may need.

Be sure to keep your capabilities statement up to date. As your contract portfolio grows, list the growing and improving references accordingly.

Does the Government Buy What you Are Selling?

The first fundamental question is whether there is a government market for what you are trying to sell. The question can be more complicated than one would think to answer. Despite political rhetoric about "limited government," the American federal and state governments are vast in scope, with tens of millions of employees and nearly 100,000 political subdivisions, agencies, departments, bureaus, and quasi-government organizations. People in my line of work intentionally only focus on our narrow areas of expertise because, frankly, the market size is incomprehensible.

Research

For the federal government, freely accessible tools are provided that work quite well. I will first mention the Federal Procurement Data System, or FPDS, accessible at www.fpds.gov. FPDS provides an interface and summarized contract award records, generally in the form of purchase orders. It may take practice to search the papers with its interface efficiently, but you should be able to quickly see (or not) if there is an existing public sector market demand.

Searching for a business name is easier than looking for specific purchased products. The purchase orders usually are [very] summarized and quantities are often challenging to determine, and specifications or details are rare. My trick is to identify several very similar competitors and look for those companies in the FPDS records. Once you have a stack of competitors' purchase orders, you may have enough to piece together products and services of interest, the buyers, and how much they spend.

Pro Tip: Research the frequency of purchases by each agency, and look for patterns of "when" they buy. Develop a plan to approach them about six months ahead of the next anticipated purchase timeframe.

The Competition

The government sales and services marketplace is very competitive. The larger contract sizes inherent to government opportunities will draw high-quality sales and business development professionals. These are not the corner used car lot salespeople, and these are professionals that have made it through the initial contracting "hoops" that you are striving to do. They have developed the skills, networks, and a message for a compelling offer to the government. Don't underestimate them.

Please don't misunderstand; I, more than most, recognize entrepreneurs as the A-Players that bring their best game onto the field. Being an entrepreneur means that if you are not successful, you don't eat, so it's easy to develop self-confidence in your skills. Unlike the commercial market, where your customer is looking at one, two, or maybe three offers, including yours, a government customer might be looking at a dozen or more.

Here's a secret, around 90% of companies that obtain a basic Federal Supply Schedule award will never win a single government contract. However, if you align the 90% to the number that never attempts to market to government agencies and never submit a qualified proposal, there will be significant overlap.

Government sales are not very difficult, but it does require practice, patience, and a bit of tenacity.

Pro Tip: Never underestimate the quality of your competition. Public sector sales and contracting is a challenging and technical process and industry. The market naturally attracts very high quality professionals. Always assume the next person is at least as good as you are, and bring your best game every time.

What do you Do Well?

Now, we will talk about how you can be one of the 10% that are successful in the public sector marketplace, some secrets for getting started, and lucrative tricks of the trade.

Avoid looking like "all things to all people." You may have many skills, but you are not at your best at all of them. Trying to do so will make you appear to the government as the "jack of all trades and master of none," which is not a good position. Allow me to illustrate with the following short story.

Joe's Quick Lube Shop

Years ago, Joe used to work on cars in high school shop class, helping out his friends, and with his father in the garage, and he continues to tinker with a hobby car. He may even do a few car repairs on the side for cash.

Professionally, Joe owns an auto parts retailer that sells auto parts, tires, and car batteries and offers light vehicle servicing. Late one Saturday night, while perusing new federal business opportunity postings on Sam.gov, Joe finds a recent solicitation for the local US Forest Service division in Montana requesting proposals for diesel mechanic service at remote locations in the region. The requirement is probably fixing fire trucks, bulldozers, and other heavy equipment while supporting fire crews in remote areas during the fire season each year. Theoretically, Joe could hire a few diesel mechanics and buy some heavy equipment to put tracks back on bulldozers or whatever else they need, but how does this look to the contracting officer evaluating Joe's proposal?

Joe makes a great business selling car batteries and changing the oil on Subarus with unskilled and semi-skilled staff, but does he have a credible plan to recruit and retain certified diesel experts with experience in the bush? Will he know what equipment and supplies he will need to forward deploy on-site, or does he even know "how much he doesn't know"? Sure, he may figure it out through trial and error, but the first season will be terrible if he can even perform.

Best Value

There is a common misconception that the government "buys from the lowest bidder." The truth is, this is not usually the case. It probably is when buying pallets of bottled water for relief supplies but not for technical or complex procurements. The government selects a vendor using many strategies, such as "Lowest Price, Technically Acceptable," "Best Value," or various formulas using risk avoidance as the primary consideration.

In this example, it is doubtful that Joe's proposal would be considered "technically qualified" to make it through the initial proposal screening. Even if it were a "lowest bid" competition, an experienced provider like Joe should never consider submitting a lowest-cost bid for something unfamiliar, particularly with high-cost tools, supplies, and remote travel involved. If Joe were to win the contract award somehow, he would be required to perform, even if losing a great deal of money.

The Competition

Using Joe's example, Joe's competitors for the opportunity are two regional dealerships that provide on-site services for diesel heavy equipment lessees and owners. Their existing field maintenance diesel mechanics have fully outfitted heavy-duty trucks, specialized tools, winches, and maybe a bucket lift. Their quote pricing is 17% and 23% higher than Joe's. Both include resumes of their supervisory mechanic staff, resumes for the technicians assigned to the contract, specific replacement part prices and inventories on hand, and copies of the technicians' manufacturer certifications.

Which one would you pick?

Likely Outcome

The contracting officer will disqualify Joe's bid as non-responsive or unqualified. They will either award it to the next-lowest priced competitor or submit a Best and Final Offer or "BAFO" request to both remaining offers, letting them know they are the "final two" or "best two offers" and ask for their best price.

Lemonade Instead of Lemons

To compete more effectively, it's always better for Joe to stay within his swim lane. Endlessly writing proposals for opportunities he will never win is not a credible strategy to pursue. It draws attention and resources from developing other sales opportunities that better suit his capabilities while discouraging his proposal and bid team.

Many federal, state, and local fleet management sections contract with local providers to provide general vehicle maintenance services, for example, regular oil service maintenance on police cars. Joe's already-existing staff, facility, and experience will allow him to bid a very reasonable price on these opportunities with high confidence in turning a respectable profit. After being awarded the contract, Joe can add a few more "junior technicians" to perform the easy tasks and do even better financially.

Midway through the contract, the local police department asks Joe if he would be amicable to modifying the agreement to include some recently acquired military surplus Mine Resistant Ambush Protected vehicles (MRAPs) granted to them from the Department of Defense for their Special Weapons and Tactics (SWAT) team. Joe has two options to consider; he can determine the cost to add a certified technician to meet the requirement and the specialized vehicle lift equipment needed to lift the trucks and amortize that cost into the police department's contract modification with a margin for profitability. Or he can call one of the local diesel heavy equipment dealers mentioned above and ask them for a price as a subcontractor to do the new work. Doing so also assumes the risk that he will retain the contract after it expires in two years.

The safest option (financially) for Joe may be to take the subcontracted price quote from the diesel heavy equipment dealer, add a 15% margin to it for the same profit target he had in mind if doing the work himself, and send the modification proposal to the police department. Whenever the MRAP comes in, and it may be very seldom, Joe ships it over to the subcontractor, gets the work done quickly and competently, sends the bill to the police department, and pockets the markup. The expert subcontractor may even find additional recommendations and work needed on the truck, all with the same 15% margin, and Joe makes much more than he would have to do "the minimums" himself. With the other 159 hours left in his 160-hour schedule each month, he can focus on the things that make him [much more] money.

What Should Joe Do?

If Joe picks the first option, hiring a diesel mechanic, he may get some work here and there for his diesel technician. Still, it is more likely that he will be paying the diesel specialist a large salary to stand around and wait for the MRAP to roll in for an oil change a couple of times a year while doing other work that the junior-level staff can do.

Assuming Joe takes the low-risk, high-reward "Plan B" and subcontracts the work to the local diesel heavy equipment dealership, over the remaining two years of the contract, Joe will gain some valuable experience understanding what is needed to maintain the vehicles, the costs, and staffing required while developing the police department as a reference client in the specialized line of work.

Joe Makes the Right Choice

Fast forward to the end of the two remaining years of Joe's contract. The police department issues a re-compete Request for Proposal (RFP) for Joe's contract, including the previously added diesel work and the general gas-engine maintenance he has primarily been doing to their complete satisfaction. Joe knows his other "fast lube" competitors in the area won't consider bidding on the MRAP maintenance, so he now comfortably increases his price a little for his proposal for the next five years of services. The contracting officer has also given his company high marks for turnaround times, the accuracy of the work, and customer service.

Swim Lane

For the next five years, he comfortably proposes pricing that will average 25% net margins across the board, emphasizing in his proposal, "Joe's Quick Lube will continue to provide the police department unparalleled customer service, turnaround times, and technical performance, making our proposal the lowest-risk option for local law enforcement mission readiness." Joe's offer will likely be the only one considered responsive and technically qualified because he is the only one with the combination of light vehicle service and the occasional heavy diesel maintenance under one roof.

The US Forest Service contract is re-competed two years later. This time, Joe has his existing subcontractor relationship with the local diesel heavy equipment dealer performing the US Forest Service requirements as a prime contractor. It may be worth Joe's picking up the phone to ask the diesel heavy equipment dealer if they can use any help to bring their price down by letting Joe's team take on any gas-engine work that comes up at a lower cost than using their diesel field mechanics.

Maintaining a valuable relationship and not stepping out of one's core product or service markets is called "Staying in the Swim Lane." Usually, you make more money by doing so. I will address subcontracting in detail later in Chapter 7, Planning to Win.

PART II

SELLING TO THE
GOVERNMENT

4

OPPORTUNITIES AT DIFFERENT LEVELS OF GOVERNMENT

T he complexity of selling to the government will vary by the type of agency, relative population (or constituent) size, and "big" or "small" government culture.

Differences in procurement styles exist between federal, state, and local governments and so-called "quasi-governmental" organizations, such as water and power utilities, conservation commissions, education, and transit agencies.

Federal Opportunities

Opportunities with the federal government will take five primary forms. An open market solicitation that anyone can bid (if registered on Sam.gov), a Government-Wide Acquisition Contract (GWAC), an Indefinite Delivery/Indefinite Quantity contract (IDIQ), a Blanket Purchase Agreement (BPA), a socio-demographic set-aside, or a sole-source procurement.

The Federal Acquisition Regulation (FAR) governs US federal government procurement. Review it, read sections of interest and relevance to your business, and become familiar with it in terms of understanding how to search for and find answers quickly. Take the time to understand what is in the FAR and read the summaries of each section. You do not need to be a master of it, but having familiarity with the content will always be an advantage. The federal acquisition website is the easiest way to skim the regulation. You can find it at https://www.acquisition.gov/browse/index/far, or use your favorite search engine and search for "Federal Acquisition Regulation."

If you think the advice of a legal professional may be necessary for your case, look for someone experienced explicitly with the FAR. Government procurement is a seemingly rare area of expertise for attorneys. I don't get the impression that it is part of the normal curriculum in law schools. Naturally, attorneys in Washington, DC, or northern Virginia will usually have experience and familiarity with government contracts than the average lawyer in Oregon or Hawaii. Note that another set of regulations overlays the FAR for defense-related contracting, known as the "DFAR."

State Opportunities

US states' governments are similar to the US federal government with varying levels of complexity ranging from "very easy," all procurements are full & open market, to complex combinations of pre-competed contracting vehicles and socioeconomic set-asides similar to the federal government.

Unlike the federal government, state-level socioeconomic set-aside programs will only apply to qualifying companies within the state's boundaries.

Local Government Opportunities

Local governments are problematic, in my opinion, compared to other layers of government. Counties are funded by property tax assessments, federal and state healthcare reimbursements, local sales taxes, and airport/seaport fees. From my observations, County governments are better funded and, while still somewhat quirky, will tend to have more money to spend than their "city" cohabitants.

City government budgets usually consist of a police and fire department that consumes about 80% of their resources, and they do everything else on 20% or less. Digging deeper, they are more accurately described as retirement and pension fund operator with "police & fire services" on the side.

If you sell tires for police cars or fire trucks, or tactical gear for law enforcement, they are your target customer. It can be tough to find your niche in city government procurements for most other vendors that specialize in goods or services for federal or state government agencies. If you do, pricing will usually be an uncomfortable topic.

Utility and school districts will generally have better procurement opportunities than other local government agencies. Each of these will have reasonably competitive procurement processes, generally buying many goods and services, and is usually disconnected from local politics.

Marketing and Sales Rules

The federal government and the states have established contracting and administration regulations, rules, laws, and guidelines. These are not something to ignore. Not observing them can lead to a bid disqualification or even the revocation of an award protested by one of your competitors.

My recommendation is to familiarize yourself with the FAR "first." Familiarity with the FAR will make the other layers of government seem pretty simple, and you only need to note the nuances mentally. For the FAR, there is also the convenience of a single document to review that is easily accessible online.

If you are only focusing on a single state government, by all means, start with that state's procurement manual. Familiarity with the FAR will make you a better contractor overall because conditions often have inconsistencies within their policies, outcomes of "political regime changes" over the decades, and administrations' varying levels of competency over the years.

Examples and Suggestions

I have a few basic rules that illustrate the differences between working with the government and any other prospective commercial customer:

1. You can't buy gifts, dinners, drinks, travel, or conference admissions for your government customers, employees, or contracting officers. Be sure to verify, but most states and the federal government generally allow minor incidentals, such as buying coffee and bringing some donuts when sitting down for a meeting. Avoid anything beyond a gesture of hospitality. If meeting offsite for coffee, I'll offer to pay, and they almost always decline.

2. There are some exceptions to this rule that anyone may encounter. Often, I develop friendships over time among my customers. The companies usually last well beyond the contractual relationship and are no longer business-oriented. I'll let them take the lead, but taking turns buying the beer is a social norm. If it's personal and not related to a procurement underway, it's only human, and many of us develop friendships at work. Don't insist and don't do elaborate gifts, trips, or dinners, or you can inadvertently create a problem for yourself later.

3. After I finish the contract, I let the friendship continue if welcomed. My customers are all well aware of the ethics regulations, so it has never been a problem in my past, and I think they respect the arms' length distance I practice. I

assume the practice has been accepted because I've never been asked to change it, and I have never found myself in an uncomfortable situation. In short, there is strict adherence to the regulations, and then there is being "socially awkward." I stick to the rules, but I'm also social and enjoy knowing my customers and coworkers.

Ethical Standards

In addition to regulations that govern the marketing and sales activities of contractors, ethical standards are also imposed.

Family Members

You must disclose any conflicts of interest. You must notify the prospective customer if you have a family member working with the prospective government agency customer. It usually won't have a negative effect when disclosed and mitigated, but you may be prohibited from working on-site after a contract award. This happened to me once. My relative wasn't associated with the contract opportunity or the work's subject matter, and it was only regarded as an agency policy decision. We didn't lose the contract; I couldn't personally work on it.

If you conceal your connection and win the contract, any competitor with three brain cells to rub together will have fantastic grounds to protest the award. If you have a spouse or close family member in the contracting unit or is a project sponsor, in the organizational management, or in any position of influence over the vendor selection, don't submit a bid unless you disclose and receive permission in advance. Your family member should completely recuse themselves from the process.

Take an Ethics Class if You Haven't Already

Understand your ethical obligations and restrictions. If you previously worked for the government, there are usually minimum periods "post-employment" during which you cannot solicit or conduct any business with the agency.

Normally, a "cone of silence" will be imposed during the solicitation. Once an RFP or RFQ is published, only the contracting officer representing the agency for the solicitation can communicate with prospective vendors. Respect this process and keep your communication points of contact to only the contract officer and his or her designated representatives.

Doing Business with the Federal Government

I prefer doing business with the US federal government to all other levels of government. I think initial success with federal opportunities from a few past performance references is easier to reach. It can take longer because of the slowness of the systems and processes involved, but most new contractors will see better results over the first two years when compared to the equivalent level of effort with state and local government entities.

Starting up a federal government contracting business will generally yield some revenue results within 12 months if you have a competitive company, a product, or a service of interest and are competent in your business development efforts. Qualifying for small business, veteran-owned, or socioeconomic certifications will considerably improve your odds. The positive of starting with federal contracting is that the contract sizes are usually larger. State and local operations "may" see results within the same first year, but it is probably a lower percentage of the companies that do, and typically, the revenue size for each contract will be smaller.

There are other reasons to prefer doing business with the Federal Government:

1. Stability of revenue. The federal government likes to buy in three, four, and five-year intervals. I sell it once, and we get income for the next five years as long as we do our jobs right.
2. Level of effort. It takes about as much time and effort to write a formal response to a solicitation for a $5,000 RFP from a local government as it does to make a $500,000 sale to the Federal Government. It looks good if I make one $2 million deal with a large federal agency. If I am doing the $5,000 state stuff, I need to bid and win 40 times in the same year to reach the same revenue targets. Do I turn down the small stuff? No, but I don't prioritize my research time looking for them.
3. I appreciate the business style of the federal customers. The federal procurement process is well documented, regulated, trained, and professional. If I have a compelling offer, good experience, competitive pricing, and a relationship with the customer, I will have a high expectation of getting the contract, and I often do.

A downside of doing business with the federal government is the higher competitiveness among the other contractors. Your federal market competitors have the same motivations as you do, and about 10% of them will become very good at winning new business on average. Of course, there are ways to beat them, and we will talk about this in Chapter 7, Planning to Win.

A second downside is the customer's level of sophistication in the federal market. The federal government contracts much of its operations, and the procurement team is highly experienced. You will need to know what you are doing to be successful.

Researching your competitors is a skill you will need. We will also discuss this more in Chapter 7, Competition.

Doing Business with State Governments

There are fundamental differences to remember when comparing federal and state government opportunities or contemplating where you will allocate your resources.

First, I expect the sales effort to be more difficult at a state or local level than a federal version with an identical requirement. If comparing two opportunities of similar scope between a federal agency versus the state or local market, the level of effort for the state and local opportunity will usually be higher.

Second, there isn't a way to put this politely, but newcomers to the public sector should have some early warning so as not to be taken aback. I have seen some wacky stuff in some state procurement solicitations. In California, you will need to stipulate in a standardized form (for each solicitation) that you do not do business in Darfur, the African nation of Sudan. If you are, there is even a waiver process to seek written permission from the Department of General Services if you are doing business in Darfur but still want to submit a bid for a State of California opportunity. The Darfur form is filed for every offer from every vendor. I have always wanted to ask how many prospective companies this affects and if it is worth killing hundreds of trees to reproduce the form for every bid, proposal, and quote submitted by contractors for every State of California opportunity each year. Does the nation of Sudan have a genuine interest in contracting with small IT companies based in Sacramento? Are many family owned construction firms based in Darfur bidding on some curb & gutter work for the California Department of Transportation in Los Angeles? With its higher cost of living, regulation, and tax rates, California companies will struggle to compete in Ohio, let alone in Darfur.

Third, so as not to think that I am picking on a "blue" state instead of a "red" one - I can criticize a red('ish) one too. Wisconsin requires bidders to certify they are not boycotting the Nation of Israel. I'm not anti-Semitic, but I don't know exactly how I could [or not] "boycott" Israel. I haven't been to Israel, I would like to go, and it's on the bucket list, but I haven't been there to spend money yet. Technically, does that mean that I am boycotting Israel? If I win a contract and a competitor is disappointed and protests my eligibility to have been selected, could they allege I was boycotting Israel because I haven't been there or because I haven't submitted a bid (in Hebrew) for a contracting opportunity in Israel? One can see how some of these "feel good" types of documents can create a legal pitfall.

Fourth, many states have a "local preference," giving a 5% or other nominal pricing preference to bidders headquartered within their boundaries. This one is easy to understand. Local businesses employ the state's residents and contribute to the tax base. The employees pay taxes in addition to whatever taxes the company pays directly.

It's vital to identify preferential competitive advantages [or disadvantages] immediately when planning a response. If you are in an industry where you can't pull 5% out of your price to remain competitive with an in-state offer, you may want to reconsider the effort to produce a bid or at least calibrate your expectations of success a little lower.

Fifth, the last comment I will make about state governments is that many are not as transparent in their evaluation and contract awards as the federal government. While I wouldn't call it corruption because I don't have direct evidence, I have anecdotal examples. For example, I lost an award by 0.20 points out of a 500-point evaluation scorecard. On another occasion, I was told, "No, you can't bid on this because only this [other] contractor will need to win this time, but we'll give you the next one." I have also received an award for a $2.5 million contract in writing via a fax machine (dating myself somewhat), only to see the award rescinded several days later because another vendor forgot to submit their offer. It was already a month after the solicitation closing date, and the other vendor didn't attend the "mandatory" bidders' conference either. These examples are not from the same state; these are examples from separate ones.

Sixth, the "scope of work" will vary (generally) between state and federal government agencies. For the most part the federal government writes checks and monitors the performance of the programs it is paying for. The US Department of Transportation, for example, is not building roads. The Centers for Medicare and Medicaid are not reviewing and approving individual claims. Generally, federal agencies provide funding and specifications to each state, and the states build the highways. The military, NASA, NOAA, CDC, federal judiciary, and the FBI are a few of the obvious exceptions.

State government agencies will do more of what people think of as government services. They will define the programs, add state-provided funds to them, and direct local requirements.

If you want to do business with state governments, invest your time, develop relationships, and be the vendor they prefer. If you are not developing the relationships beforehand and doing some marketing before releasing the solicitation, you may be wasting your time. The evaluation and scoring tend to be a bit "arbitrary" at the state levels, so only being the best value, lowest bid or highest-quality product or service offered won't guarantee a leg up on the competition.

***

Cities and Counties

Although I group cities and counties as local governments, they operate somewhat differently from one another. I'll convey some differences in generalities to set your expectations with; they are by no means universal truths.

Counties (or parishes) will usually have better sources of revenue than cities. The counties collect property taxes, airport and port fees, court fees, restitution, dog licenses, and other recurring payments. They spend a lot but will also have better cash flow than city governments do.

Cities commonly have less-stable sources of revenue in comparison, sources such as sales taxes, hotel taxes, speeding and parking tickets, some revenue share from the county, and taxes on venue tickets. There are many others, but analyzing government funding sources is not my intent here. My point is to highlight some of the differences so readers can set better expectations and devise winning strategies.

My reasoning is based on the prior research and analysis of the financial statements for cities and counties. Many are buried in their employee salaries, benefits, and pension costs for promises made years ago and now coming due.

There are three upsides to doing business with a city or county. The first is if it is **your** city or county. You have the home court advantage, and it's something you can do without adding any cost or resources to your business. If you provide a service that they must have and are currently buying, you may be able to do it for a much lower cost and make some friends in city hall. You may only need your regular sales and service people, you won't incur additional salary costs, and you pick up a prestigious local customer.

The second reason is to establish past performance references. If you need viable and documented references for state or federal government proposals and only have some commercial ones, picking up local agencies before moving on to a state, and federal contracting enterprise is an excellent strategy.

And third, local governments are where the rubber meets the road for government services. They provide social services, law enforcement, and other high-touch government services. This is your primary public sector vertical if your product or service is in demand at a local physical level.

How Are You Going to Make Your Sale?

Government entities cannot walk into a store and buy something off the shelf (usually). Public procurement regulations require competition to select the best product or service at the lowest cost to the taxpayers under the required terms and conditions.

Various methods for fair and open competition have been established to comply with public procurement regulations, and I'll describe the most common ones here.

Full and Open Opportunities

The first type of government business transaction that we will discuss is a full and open solicitation and will only require essential vendor registration in the state or agency's procurement management system. Typically this is the only requirement for a "full and open" bid to be submitted and considered by the buyer.

Expect to provide information such as your employer identification number (EIN), address, licensing information, NAICS codes, and financial statements. These are usually only essential informational registrations with the government entity or central procurement authority.

Full and open opportunities are primarily responded to in the form of a proposal or quotation in response to a Request for Proposal (RFP), Request for Quote (RFQ), Invitation to Negotiate (ITN), or Request for Bid (RFB). The full and open transactions are what newcomers to the public sector contracting industry will think of in terms of doing business with the government, but depending on which statistic one looks at, it ranges from only about 10% to 15% of the total purchases made by various levels of government.

Multi-State Procurement Vehicles

The National Association of State Procurement Officials (NASPO) has organized a cooperative contracting system called ValuePoint. ValuePoint solicits and awards contracts for a variety of goods and services. Nearly all (or all) of the US states and territories participate in NASPO, and it can be an effective shortcut to gain market access in the participating states with reduced effort. At a minimum, the NASPO contract award and price schedule can be used as a public sector reference for other contracts awarded by individual states, such as California's Multiple Award Schedule (CMAS).

Each contract solicited and awarded by NASPO ValuePoint is at the discretion of each member state to adopt or not. Member states do not have to participate in all, or any, ValuePoint contracts, but they can also change their mind along the way. If a state opts in, it can add its overlays of terms and conditions to each contract holder by use of a participating addendum (PA).

In my experience, working with NASPO contracts for almost five years, few states' centralized contracting departments will adopt a contractor's NASPO award until one of the state's agencies asks them to do so. The PA forms are elementary, a few pages at most, but there is often political resistance to doing so, and they usually take longer than one would think reasonable to have executed.

Nonetheless, NASPO is an effective tool if your product or service is within the scope of work for a NASPO solicitation. I regard one of the annual NASPO events, NASPO Exchange, as one of the best trade shows for the public sector market and certainly the best for state government.

For more information, visit www.naspovaluepoint.org.

I consider NASPO ValuePoint a form of cooperative contracting, which I will cover in more detail later in this chapter.

Single-State Government Contracting Vehicles

Single-state procurement vehicles will usually be less complex than federal versions. These are solicited, negotiated, and awarded by a single state for their use. From my observations, they mirror a federal equivalent, such as a GSA schedule contract; many will require the submittal of the vendor's GSA schedule with the state's cover documents.

Why not use a multi-state procurement vehicle or a federal cooperative contract? I think it is the industrial funding fees, the contracts usually incur a 0.75% supportive fee to be paid by the vendor, and the state is looking to avoid the perceived higher cost. However, the states charge a fee of their own for their contract vehicles, so it is a matter of who gets the payment, I suppose.

Pre-Requisites

Many federal and state procurement solicitations will require (or "leverage") a procurement vehicle (contract) for their requirement. The use of these vehicles is commonly known as a "simplified acquisition." The concept of a procurement vehicle is for the procuring authority to hold a competition for a limited number of contract awards ahead of actual need to be used later for anticipated future requirements. For example, a state may solicit and award contracts for snow removal during the summer months. The state knows it will need snow removal, but it cannot specify where or when.

These are also referred to as "pre-competed contract awards," "multiple award schedules," or "Indefinite Delivery Indefinite Quantity" (IDIQ) contracts. Florida often requires the use of a previously awarded federal GSA schedule contract. California uses the California Multiple Award Schedule (CMAS) and the California IT Master Services Agreement (MSA) for technology products and services. Texas has "TXMAS" (Texas Multiple Award Schedule). There are others.

For states that prefer to use these pre-competed multiple award vehicles, you will need to first win an award on one of their accepted contracting vehicles before using it to pursue bidding opportunities or partner with another firm that already has a professional services teammate or product supplier.

It is important to note that for states managing multiple contract vehicles, the holder of one vehicle cannot bid on an opportunity that is solicited to a different vehicle, so you may find yourself obtaining several contracting vehicle awards within the same state or just picking the best fit and only focus on your relevant opportunities. Some firms will secure one and team with another firm that has another, sharing each other's positions.

For extra "fun," some states have "tiers" within these multiple award schedules. The tier determines the maximum contract size for which the contractor can submit a bid. Research and thoroughly understand your state's requirements or call and request an appointment with the contracting officer listed as the point of contact on the schedule's solicitation materials. I have always found contracting professionals to be very helpful. Just be polite and respectful of their time, and they will do so for you.

Easier Options

For the most part, conservative-leaning states with smaller governments will (but not always) trend toward full and open solicitations, so getting started with the red states is easier and a little quicker on average. Unfortunately, these smaller governments also equate to fewer business opportunities.

Other Types of Simplified Procurements

Most levels of government employ some of many pre-competed approaches to routine acquisitions. To address all of these approaches would be an exhaustive effort. Instead, I will discuss the most common ones. Consider these as examples and understand that they all work fundamentally in the same way. The intent is the same, to streamline the procurement process by evaluating the contractors' qualifications or pricing periodically in advance of anticipated continuing needs, and to filter out bidders that would be unlikely to perform the contract reliably.

For the solicitations leveraging these procurement vehicles, only bidders holding the minimum required contract are permitted to place a bid for the period that the contract is in effect or the contract's term.

Procurement vehicles are normally a multiyear contract term, and the generic terms and conditions usually allow for economic adjustment, or "escalation," of each contractor's pricing offer. The most common is an annual adjustment equal to or lower than the yearly Consumer Price Index (CPI) reported by a specific source, but any index can be offered or suggested. It is up to the Contracting Officer, regulation, and legislation to accept the proposal.

IDIQ

The first of the "others" that I'll describe is the agency-IDIQ, or indefinite delivery, indefinite quantity. These are often used for recurring business requirements, but no specific ongoing need exists. There is no guarantee of how much may be ordered from the vendor, if any, or how often. These are usually solicited and awarded for a period of years, a base term or period, followed by one or more optional extension periods. Five-year terms are prevalent; a one-year base period with four 1-year optional extensions. Bidders are usually asked to submit "ceiling pricing" that would be appropriate for the minimum order quantity of whatever the product or service is. These awards are generally granted to multiple winners, so the specific follow-on requests for quotations (RFQs) can also become competitive. Contractors are free to offer discounts on the specific jobs as they come up, but the quoted cost cannot exceed the initially awarded agreement "ceiling price" per unit of work.

Consider the example of a public works road-repair contract for emergency snow removal. There is no way for the agency to predict how much work will be needed in the next year; it could be a mild winter or a daily white-out. The purpose is to identify qualified prospective contractors, negotiate pricing and contractual terms acceptable to both parties, establish insurance or bonding requirements, and sign the contract awards in advance of the emergency needs. As work is required, requests for quotes are issued with short notice, and the selected bidder(s) will be issued "task orders" for the work to be performed, using the prior-negotiated terms, conditions, and pricing. Expenses are commonly reimbursable above the contract performance price and terms for travel or other requirements associated with a specific task order. Examples may be airline travel, per diem expense allowances, mobilization costs per day for roadwork projects, or many other possibilities. These are complexities defined and negotiated within the contracting vehicle, and the value for both parties is a streamlined purchasing experience.

For the new contractor starting out in a market dominated by multi-year IDIQ procurement vehicles, it will mean acting as a subcontractor on someone else's contract award or looking for other opportunities until the prevailing contracting vehicle expires and is replaced with a new IDIQ solicitation and competition.

Government-Wide Acquisition Contracts

Government-Wide Acquisition Contracts (GWACs) are federal contracting vehicles that operate similarly to the agency IDIQ above but will span multiple agencies or the entire government to access and use the contract for several years. For example, GSA's Alliant and the follow-on Alliant 2 were prominent GWACs used by the federal government for various business requirements. These served a large percentage of the federal healthcare information technology services anticipated. Both were awarded to the highest-scoring pool of contractors out of hundreds of offers received and were subsequently used for the next ten years to meet business requirements. For a five-year federal services contract arising from the associated task orders, the winners were guaranteed the opportunity to compete for a stream of work to be performed over the next fifteen years against a relatively small number of possible competitors. For illustration, contract holders could theoretically fulfill task orders issued late in the tenth year of the contract for years 11-15 since the award date). For the contracting officers, the advantage is to offer complex solicitation opportunities to a reasonably sized pool of highly-qualified companies and have fewer resulting offers to evaluate. They may receive five or six excellent offers to consider and negotiate versus dozens to read with full and open solicitations, of which 10% or 20% might be regarded as responsive. The government sees the use of a GWAC for simplified procurement as a labor and process-time saver.

Blanket Purchase Agreements

Blanket Purchase Agreements (BPAs) are a commonly used Federal procurement tool but are also seen at state and local levels. BPA's are similar to an agency IDIQ or GWAC but are less formal and often a "single award" - a single winner rather than multiple awardees. That single contractor will then be given an unspecified future volume of business at the negotiated price and terms.

For example, air passenger transportation requirements might be solicited as a BPA. Major airlines respond to solicitations for proposals for a three or five-year contract. Each airline aggregates its partner community to ensure worldwide travel services or the coverage specified and prepares an offer that includes an elaborate station-to-station rate table, a cost per passenger per mile, or whatever the pricing specification is. The government may be able to provide estimates based on historical purchasing, but specific future volumes are impossible to know.

Multiple Award Schedules

The last type I will discuss is the multiple award schedules. The federal government and many states use these tools. In short, these resemble catalogs. The contractors offer their goods or services, the product or service specifications, the associated costs, and any capabilities required for the offer. Some schedule offers can be complex to assemble. GSA's Federal Supply System (FSS) Schedule series would be one example of a challenging package to develop. While the product or service descriptions, price sheets, and other inclusions are more complex than is probably needed, it is essential to be aware that the business documentation required is also substantial, with a high level of attention to detail necessary to be successful.

Leveraged Procurements

I have observed some leveraged procurement contracts at the city and county levels. In recent memory, the City of Phoenix has a pre-competed contract vehicle for technology services provided to the City of Phoenix and Sky Harbor airport, for example. I'm sure there are many others, and I encourage readers to identify their targets of interest and research their local market for making a market entry.

There are about 39,000 municipalities in the United States, and I have briefly discussed only a handful. Use these basic examples as a starting point and conduct some research of your hometown, now understanding what you looking at and how you can approach your target.

Pro Tip: Procurement vehicles are not solicited very often, try to submit an offer whenever the opportunity presents itself.

Pro Tip: If lacking other government references for your public sector proposals, try using a combination of commercial references with procurement vehicle contract awards.

Cooperative Contracting

Another tool for doing business with state governments is a US Federal GSA schedule, known as the Federal Supply Schedule system (FSS). Many GSA schedules are cooperative, meaning that if you agree, state and local governments can use them. Doing so is at the discretion of the state or local government. For states that do not honor GSA schedules directly, such as California or Texas, the state will reference your company's awarded GSA schedule terms, conditions, and pricing in their equivalent contract. Other states, such as Florida, buy from GSA schedules directly.

Some states will opt into or cooperate with the contracts written by other state governments. Where this is customary, as a hypothetical example, an agreement signed in, for example, Texas may be reutilized later the same year by Nebraska to procure the same products or services, with the terms and conditions and pricing awarded by Texas, but skipping Nebraska's competitive procurement process. Several states do this; others commonly use Minnesota's contracts, for example.

Procurement Vehicles, Last Thoughts

Remember, the valid term of service for a multiple award schedule, IDIQ, GWAC, or BPA, will be longer than the date of expiration stated on your award. The reason is that the contractor can bid and win a contract through the last day of the term of the multiple-award agreement. The period of performance for that contract would then extend beyond the award expiration date of the underlying multiple-award agreement.

For example, if Company A holds an award for GSA's Alliant 2 in March of 2017 and the award states an expiration date of March 2027. In January of 2027, Company A wins a task order opportunity specifying work for the subsequent five years, beginning in February 2027 and ending in 2032. The performance period for that task order would start in February of 2027 and continue through January or February of 2032. During its performance, Company will also be subject to the terms, conditions, and pricing submitted in March 2017, through February 2032, for the performance of the January 2027 task order.

As mentioned above, procurement vehicle pricing usually allows for annual pricing schedule escalations, protecting the contractors and ensuring the contracting vehicle's relevance over the years.

Quasi-Government Entities

In addition to the federal, state, and local government departments and agencies, public education, special districts, utilities, governance boards, professional licensing authorities, public utilities, and transportation systems are normally subject to public procurement rules.

Education

Education organizations can be excellent customers if your product or services interest them. I regard marketing to them as the most effortless government sales process. I do so for various reasons but suffice it to say they do not have the same level of oversight (or bureaucratic encumbrance) as the others. Many school districts and universities operate more like private entities.

Private schools are not funded by the government and are considered private businesses; whether organized as a non-profit and supported by a faith-based organization or operating as a for-profit organization, neither is subject to public procurement laws. I mention this because if you are successfully selling products or services for a public school district or university, remember that the private ones will probably have many similar needs. Many large private universities conduct their procurements similarly to public ones but without the same level of transparency.

Cooperative Contracts in Education

I have not observed pre-competed procurement vehicles in k-12 education.

University-level education is a different matter. Public universities are often part of a "university system" for the state where they are located. Generally, they are split into three types, community colleges, state universities, and universities of "systems." Three separate contracting and solicitation advertisement systems are likely in place within each state.

Many colleges, state universities, and university systems use a system of pre-competed contracting. I am familiar with California and North Dakota, representing opposite ends of the system spectrum so I will use these as examples.

California's university system is governed by the University of California Office of the President (UCOP). UCOP functions as a centralized procurement for all of the Universities of California. California State University procurements are handled by the CSU chancellor's office and published in California's procurement advertising. Both systems use a pre-competed vendor contracting program.

North Dakota, in my opinion, works better, although I am biased as a UND graduate school alumnus. The University of North Dakota research university system and the North Dakota State University System procurements are full and open procurement systems.

My anecdotal observation is large population and "blue" states will have pre-competed (protected) market procurements, while the generally smaller and rural (red) states will have full and open free market competition for public contracting opportunities.

Utility and Transportation Districts

Special districts also implement a form of public procurement practices. These are the various water and power utilities, sanitation districts, transit districts, fire districts, regional "councils of governments," airports, seaports, and air quality districts. There are others, but you get the concept. These public or quasi-public organizations are supported by tax dollars directly or indirectly, subject to public procurement laws and processes. How they implement those processes will vary but will be more relaxed than civil service departments and generally similar to k-12 education procurement, from my limited experience.

I bring these up because as a public sector marketing and sales professional, it is easy to miss the local water and power company.

The United Nations

There is one last form of public procurement in the United States that I will mention. I do not have any experience with the United Nations, but I have observed that they put a lot of services and supplies out for bid; it's just not in my area of expertise.

I mention it because it may be worth investigating for companies based in New York that have experience with professional services, technology services, emergency supplies, education, medical services, or anything of relevant interest to nature. I will be interested in receiving feedback from readers if they have direct experience working with the UN.

If you are interested in performing services overseas, the US military and the US State Department also conduct many procurements annually for contractor services overseas. If you are already doing so successfully, the UN could be an additional prospective customer with a similar procurement system.

5

THE PUBLIC SECTOR PROCUREMENT CYCLE

P ublic sector procurements are generally conducted in the same manner, regardless of the level of government or a quasi-public organization like a utility district. Some phases may be skipped or abbreviated for lower-value purchases, and the delegated levels of purchasing authority will vary, but the process is essentially the same universally.

For example, some agencies may skip oral interviews to buy routine supplies like new tires for fire trucks, but there would probably be oral interviews for buying the fire trucks. The agency may not request the best and final offers from the finalists to buy a few desktop software licenses but may do so for the year of videoconferencing services for thousands of employees.

Having spent most of my career in information technology managed services, I expect a lengthy procurement process for professional services versus a more simplified process for cloud software sales.

Bid or No-Bid

Before I invest significant time analyzing an opportunity, planning my proposal strategy, coming up with a win theme, or how I'll price the solution - I start with a fundamental question: "Is this winnable?"

Many contractors will bid on anything that comes in the door, which probably drives the win rate down. There is a counter-view, "If you don't bid, you will never win." "If you don't bid, you will never win," and that is true too. I walk a tightrope between the two.

My "napkin math" calculates an opportunity cost for each proposal effort. It may take many person-hours to draft a thorough and competitive written response, and what other (winnable) opportunities will go by the wayside in pursuit of the Hail Mary?

No-Bids

My philosophy is that of bidding on everything that I can be competitive on. This approach means I will look for reasons to NOT bid on the opportunity, rather than looking for reasons to do so.

I start with the "hard no" issues that will end the mental conversation with myself quickly. These are pretty easy to identify:

1. I don't know anything about the customer,
2. I don't know what problems they are trying to solve,
3. I don't sell what they are looking for,
4. Are there any show-stoppers in the sample terms & conditions,
5. Am I allowed to bid on this?

Let's discuss these briefly so you can apply them to your business.

I don't know anything about the customer, and I don't know what problems they are trying to solve.

In the commercial world, this would not be a hindrance. You can have lunch or coffee with the prospective customer and learn something about the problems they face. When selling to the government, there are limited opportunities for doing so after the solicitation becomes formalized. If a just-released RFP lands on your desk and you have not previously met with the customer, the information available to you is going to be limited to what you can glean from the RFP's background inclusions, from the research you can do on the web, and from contacts you may have that know more than you and the Q&A phase of the solicitation. That isn't a lot to go on, especially when your competitors are far ahead of you.

I don't sell what they are looking for

It may seem self-explanatory, but we should discuss this for a moment. There are arbitrage opportunities every day in the public sector marketplace. You may have the product or services the customer wants, and another company has the specified contract vehicle, or vice-versa. Often, those circumstances will make great partnerships.

If you are holding the required contract, and your prospective teammate can provide the missing products or services, you may have an opportunity to make some extra revenue by being a "market maker." We will discuss this more later.

Are there any show-stoppers in the sample terms & conditions?

Sample terms and conditions are primarily applicable when selling software or other published products, "something" as a Service, and different types of products derived from intellectual property rights. Be sure to carefully review the terms to verify that they align with any constraints you may have as a vendor.

Am I allowed to bid?

You cannot submit an offer if the opportunity is a minority-owned or woman-owned set-aside opportunity and a white male owns your company. If you do, you will be disqualified. Other constraints are typical service-disabled veteran-owned small business (SDVOSB) set-asides, sole-source procurement notifications, and in-state or in-city preferences, as other examples.

Bids

When deciding to bid can be more of a struggle to defend your reasoning:

1. Do we historically compete well against the incumbent?
2. Can I compete on cost and pricing?
3. Do I have the resources to work on this proposal versus other opportunities?
4. Does the deadline look suspicious?
5. Do I need any teammates or subcontractors to assist, and are they available?
6. Do I know who the competition will be?
7. Do I know the customer and understand their touch points?
8. What time of the year is it?

There will be a myriad of questions you will ask yourself, but these are the key ones I use. Let's discuss them briefly and how my reasoning works.

Is the incumbent a competitor we historically compete well against?

All of us have our strengths and weaknesses. If you know your competition, you may also understand what types of opportunities you usually beat them on and which you cannot. Recall the story about Joe's Quick Lube in Chapter 3. Joe couldn't prevail against the local CAT and Volvo heavy equipment dealers for a contract to provide field maintenance services for diesel-powered equipment - but he does a great job maintaining the police department's patrol cars. If the scope of work is to deliver gas engine maintenance at the contractor's shop - Joe should consider sending an offer. If the solicitation calls for the field diesel technicians discussed in Chapter 3, consider moving on.

Can I compete on cost and pricing?

Cost and pricing are multi-faceted questions to answer. If the scope of work is to be performed in Germany, your competitor already has operations in Germany, and you don't, it may be hard to compete on cost.

Within the United States, vast "cost" differences exist between geographic and political locales. Under most circumstances, a manufacturer based in California or New York with higher minimum wage, tax, regulatory, and cost of living differences for wages and salaries will have a challenging time competing with competitors based in Alabama, New Mexico, or Iowa. If you regularly compete against and lose to competitors in lower-cost jurisdictions, it may be a disadvantage you cannot overcome.

Do I have the resources?

Resource availability is a simple question to answer. If you have five proposals due next Friday, you have three proposal writers, and this opportunity adds a sixth to the pile - you may be too resource-constrained to respond to all of them. Resource availability will always estimate the deadline versus your existing workload and slack time between now and the deadline.

Does the deadline look suspicious?

We have a phrase in the public sector business. An opportunity can be "wired" for a specific vendor. By law, agencies have to re-compete their contracts periodically. But, they are often pleased with their incumbent provider, the level of service being received, and the price. They may tip the scale to their preferred (continued) solution in these cases. The unrealistically short due date will be apparent when reading the solicitation. Does it use very brand-specific terminology? Does the requirement match a competitor's catalog description of their product(s)? Or did they release the solicitation on the Wednesday afternoon before Thanksgiving, and the response is due Monday morning? You may be wasting your time if some of those criteria are present.

Do I need any teammates or subcontractors to assist, and are they available?

Some solutions require collaboration with your supply chain to respond adequately, and sometimes your partners are already over-burdened with other requirements. A lack of assistance from your teammates can impact your ability to bid, particularly for a public works construction project.

Do I know who the likely competition will be?

I usually do not learn much (or anything) from attending a bidders' conference - but I go whenever they are held for another reason. I like to see who the competitors are and what kinds of questions they ask.

Sometimes this works in your favor. I walked into a bidders' confer-ence once and took a seat. A few minutes later, when the executive sponsor in charge of the project walked in, we noticed each other. We used to work together years prior at another agency, and we had once been good friends. I had no idea he had moved to a new office. He walked over, and I reached out to shake his hand, and instead, he gave me a bear hug because it had been a few years. The contracting officer for the opportunity frowned, and so did all of the competition. I had been leaning toward a No-Bid but changed my mind.

Do I know the customer and understand their touch-points?

You will fit into this category when you are the incumbent and have been providing your products or services for several years. You have to win a few before gaining this advantage, but it is excellent.

What time of the year is it?

There is seasonality to government work. Contractor workloads will ebb & flow sort of on a slightly out-of-phase (delayed) sine wave pattern behind our government counterparts. The public sector contracting officers like to clear their desks (of all RFPs due to go out) before the holidays, for example, and they will tend to drop a lot of them right around Thanksgiving with a due date of the day before Christmas Eve or just after the New Year. While every other industry is enjoying an end-of-year slow time, government contracting salespeople are often very busy.

A couple of months after the enactment of the new budget year is also a busy time, typically August or September for state governments that operate from July 1 to June 30, and the same November and December for Federal agencies, having just received their new money in October.

During these predictable times of the year, you can expect to be busy with many opportunities.

I always prioritize opportunities. The opportunities with the best chance of winning or the largest revenue will be on the top of the stack. Below those, the preference will decline with opportunity size and the likelihood of winning.

I'll consider preparing proposals for the "long shot" opportunities during the slower months when I have more resource availability.

Pro Tip: Developing a healthy balance between "bid" and "no bid" decisions is an important skill to develop. Doing so will maximize the return (wins) for the level of effort invested.

Sources Sought and RFIs

Early during a public procurement cycle, the department's contracting officer will work with stakeholders within the agency's business units to identify what product or service is needed and conduct market research to identify potential suppliers. The goal usually is to develop internal cost estimates for budgeting purposes. The budgeting timeline can vary considerably, ranging from relatively brief for recurring needs with funds in place to a budget that must be requested and established before the acquisition can proceed.

Some agencies may have the flexibility to access funds from a discretionary budget, and some may generate their revenue from operations and have more direct-spend authority. Still, others may need approval from a governing agency or may require preparing a budget request and support from the legislature or the executive office. Sometimes, a large procurement in a state with a part-time legislature can take a year or two. There isn't a universal rule of thumb on this. Still, if you conduct repetitive business with a given agency or jurisdictional government, you will probably see patterns and develop your expectations.

Following the initial market research, the contracting officer may release a Sources Sought request. These are known by other names, such as a Market Information Request. The content and requested information are always similar. The agency requests information from the vendor community to identify products or services that will meet their business requirements. Other relevant information, such as the vendor's socioeconomic characteristics, large or small business size, past performance references, and a list of cooperative contracts held by the vendor, could streamline the procurement. For example, if a federal agency releases a Sources Sought for product "x," and several companies respond indicating they are small businesses with quality references and have the products listed on a GSA schedule, the contracting officer may release an RFQ to the GSA contract holders as a small-business set-aside.

The Request for Information (RFI) can be similar, identical, or very different from the Sources Sought. Often, it is the next step in the process. In my experience, RFIs are slightly more formal, with rough specifications. The RFI also gathers information about the market's available products or service providers, capabilities, security clearances, and other technical details. Federal government contract officers will also request socioeconomic information as part of the RFI response. Again, asking whether the interested vendors are Service-Disabled Veteran-Owned Small Businesses (SDVOSB), Minority Owned Enterprises, Woman-Owned Small Businesses, 8(a) disadvantaged firms, regular small business firms, or other-than-small. We will discuss socioeconomic factors in a later chapter.

Most agencies have socioeconomic participation goals or quotas, and the RFI will be used to determine whether the preferences can apply to the procurement. If the responses from potential socioeconomic set-aside groups are not sufficient in numbers to ensure adequate competition, the opportunity may be released as a "full and open" opportunity.

Responding to RFIs

When responding, answer the questions with your status as it is "today." If you need to add a subcontractor or other teammate to your eventual proposal to meet some of the capability requirements, it can be positive to indicate your intent to do so.

Remember, for typical small and medium-sized procurements for services, you should expect to do over 50% of the scope of work yourself, or you would look more viable as a subcontractor for someone else's proposal. Nonetheless, if you intend to participate as the prime or subcontractor later or are not sure yet, submit your response to the RFI. Often the answers received will serve as the starting point for conversations with the agency and may lead to invitations to privately present your products or services and attend vendor conferences and other marketing opportunities before the formal procurement solicitation is released.

My strategy includes responding to all RFIs within my capabilities to have a seat at the table later. When the vendor conferences come up, I'll attend with a strong interest as a likely prime contractor or observe who else is there if I am only interested in doing some of the work as a subcontractor. If the latter, I'll snap a picture of the sign-in sheet with my phone and use other tools and resources to reach out to the prospective primes later or talk to them after the event if the opportunity presents itself.

Federal RFIs

In responses to federal RFIs, you should include your NAICS code suggestion. While this may be your primary or an alternate claim for your business, you need to have your suggested code listed in your Sam.gov profile, so be sure to check if necessary.

Before the COVID pandemic, federal government RFIs often included a scheduled "industry day." Industry days allow vendors an opportunity to watch presentations by various agency business unit leaders, ask questions, and potentially get some follow-up face-to-face time with the contracting officer and their technical representatives with knowledge of the requirements. If the opportunity is outside the contractor's capabilities or not of interest for other reasons, the additional information is valuable in terms of time saved later to focus on other [better] opportunities. Since COVID-19, I have rarely seen these scheduled, but I hope they return as a normal part of the procurement cycle.

Your response to a federal RFI opportunity will always include your Sam.gov Unique Identifier, Dun & Bradstreet number, CAGE code, NAICS, socioeconomic designation, and a list of your cooperative contract awards. In other words, it should look like your capabilities statement plus answers to questions presented within the RFI. For example, if you are a Service-Disabled Veteran-Owned Small Business (SDVOSB), and the work can be considered within the scope of a NAICS code you have on your Sam.gov registration and considered "small" under the guidelines for the NAICS code - then the RFI

response I would prepare would prominently point out the requirement could be met by the use of an SDVOSB small-business set-
aside. If you are an 8(a) disadvantaged business, the contracting
officer can direct-award the opportunity to you without formal solicitation or competition. Of course, you will never know if you don't ask.
I always respond to RFIs of interest and put my best foot forward.

State and Local RFIs

RFIs for state and local government agencies in some cities will ask
for socioeconomic status. They may be less interested in socioeconomic status. They will focus more closely on the technical merits of
available products or services and the rough cost expectations for
establishing a budget. Considering these differences, your response
to the state or local government RFI will vary with the intended audience and the nature of the procurement.

Always respond in the format specified by the RFI, and avoid sending
pre-canned marketing brochures. Instead, include a transmittal letter
or executive summary and pitch your most persuasive arguments to
steer the procurement to your strengths and concise answers to any
questions in the RFI. I have not yet met a contracting officer who only
wanted the same marketing material they could obtain from your
website.

When the company I represent is a small business under a state or
local organization's guidelines, I indicate so. I will stop short of additional socioeconomic information unless the RFI requests it. State
and local procurements rarely have socioeconomic set-asides, but I
can list a few examples of jurisdictions where they are commonly
used. These include housing authorities, unemployment agencies,
departments of transportation, and transit authorities, all of which
receive substantial portions of their revenue from the federal government and have federal procurement guidelines "flowing down" for
projects where federal funds are used.

The technical section of my RFI responses includes the unique capabilities of the company and specific capabilities of the product or services I am offering as applied to the business requirements stated in the RFI. I may cite specific examples of where we have performed the same or similar services. If you are teaming up with another company to meet all the anticipated requirements, include a summary of your teaming partners and why you selected them.

The length of an RFI is not usually a concern unless a limit is stated in the RFI solicitation. I try to keep it to less than six pages of actual content and a couple of pages for the other collateral above. Include your socioeconomic status, NAICS, and suggested procurement strategy (to limit your potential competition in favor of your solution), and if you are interested - request an "industry day" to meet with the contracting officer.

Pro Tip: Responding to Sources Sought and RFI solicitations is important to develop a relationship with the contracting officer and agency ahead of the formal procurement.

RFI Response Writing

Good RFI responses are concise, speak to all requested requirements, and are devoid of unrelated sales fluff. I suggest a solid academic writing background for the "writers" in your organization. As a proposal writer and evaluator in my career, I confidently say that frequent spelling and grammatical errors leap off the page to the reader. Does a well-written response automatically get your company the business? Well, probably not, but it doesn't hurt, either. A poorly written document, such as one littered with noticeable spelling errors before the end of the executive summary, will subconsciously suggest a lack of attention to detail and expect a lower level of service from the offeror.

Writing skills are like any other type of skill. You get better by doing. If you don't have the budget for a dedicated writing team, get started with responding to RFIs. Thanks to the miracle of modern word processing software, you can also compensate for these shortcomings. Start using a commonly used word processor, and invest in a premium version of spelling and grammar-check software, don't rely on the free stuff inside of your writing software. Then enlist a few friends, family, or coworkers to be your review editors. Ask them to markup or mark on the paper draft the sentences and paragraphs that do not flow well, seem disorganized, or don't sound right. I also recommend using at least one person from outside your area of expertise, overuse of jargon will probably catch their attention, and that feedback is critical.

Pro Tip: RFI responses can be templated with boilerplate content and modified to fit specific solicitations. These can be great opportunities for new public sector staff to practice their response writing skills.

Government Follow-Up

Sometimes the government may reach out to some of the respondents of an RFI or Sources Sought solicitation. Doing so is typical for sizable custom-developed software projects or public works construction but will be very rare for small off-the-shelf or commodity purchases.

Bring your subject matter experts, sales, and capture teams as applicable for your organization. When you receive this kind of communication, they will likely invite you to demonstrate your products or ask your opinion on the complex project planning they are undergoing. Either way, it is an excellent opportunity to market yourself, so you will want to bring your "A" game.

Who is Going?

I will always err on the side of too many people versus not enough. I will ask how many can accompany me, and I will usually fill the limit. The people I bring will accomplish the following: answer any anticipated technical or project-related questions, listen for and understand the customer's pain points that you can weave into a future sales proposal, detailed note-taking, a program or project manager candidate if one is anticipated, and people that will be writing the proposal (typically sales).

The attendance roles often overlap with the same people, which is fine. I am discussing the pieces you should have in place at a marketing phase meeting with a prospective government customer. I don't think any of those is more or less important than another. You do need all of them represented if you can.

Your technical subject matter experts (SMEs) are a non-negotiable inclusion. You should anticipate many questions related to whatever was in your response to the RFI, and you can also expect questions about likely parts of a future scope of work that you did not address in the written response.

Business executives, analysts, and project managers are usually very good at listening to customer problems and pain points. Here, it would help if you had individuals used to hearing from a customer in the field, suggesting alternatives based on your available solutions, or communicating the need for enhancements or modifications back to your design and production teams. I have found product managers to not be very good at this, they usually have a product roadmap, and if a customer's issue skews off their plan, their first approach will be to convince the customer to change their goal (to fit their product roadmap). The next presenter comes in after you, and they take the opposite tack, listening to the customer and offering suggestions to work with their needs, and your offer is probably dead before you write it. Always put yourself in the customer's shoes. They are trying to buy a solution to their problem, not a solution to someone else's problem (and still have their problem). What you eventually choose for an approach in your future sales proposal should not be voiced at this stage, nor should you ever discuss a cost estimate (unless asked). Focus on listening.

Note-taking is more of a skill than a role. The project manager type of individual or account support professional will generally take outstanding notes for the team. It can be anyone, and I suggest the ones that turn notes into intelligence to be shared with the rest of the group, not just doodles on a notepad. I recommend using a specific person for this because of perception and your ability to collect intelligence. Few will be paying attention if everyone on your side of the table is busy scribbling down everything they hear. I will usually scratch a keyword here and there, so I remember to return to it when I have the opportunity to speak. Noting a future comment is not the same as taking meeting notes, and I think it shows professionalism. I am talking about here that 5 out of 5 people are feverishly typing away on their laptop keyboards while everyone else is subtly distracted.

Lastly, your proposal manager must be there if you have a different team for writing proposals. Nothing beats first-hand listening and interaction with the likely readers of a future proposal. A good writer will pick up on the culture, interests, and concerns of the prospective evaluators, and those concerns can be carefully woven into the document, giving a perception that the proposal "speaks to them," and that is the A+ target.

Pro Tip: Keep the headcount for a government follow-up to a reasonable size, but bring all of the expertise anticipated.

Requests for Proposal

The Request for Proposal (RFP) is the formal procurement document issued by the prospective customer. Some jurisdictions refer to it as a

Request for Quotation (RFQ), or some prefer Invitation to Negotiate (ITN). I will refer to all of these interchangeably, and I have never been able to detect a difference. If anything, an RFQ may seem a little "shorter" for a target length than the other two. However referred to, the RFP should contain all the information and specifications necessary for a contractor to draft a responsive offer.

First, a few rules of thumb. It is unrealistic to "boilerplate" all of your RFP responses. RFPs will often specify the content you will be submitting in terms of the order of the content in your response, page limits, and required supporting documents. Usually, the agency will include questions in the RFP that each bidder must answer in their response. In the technology world that I am most familiar with, these are usually in the form of yes/no feature specifications that I will typically answer in the form of a two or three-column table: RFP Question, yes/no, and comments. I aim to make the yes/no (pass/fail) questions as easy to review and score as possible. If you bury answers within extended, drawn-out paragraph writing, you risk some being missed or bore the reader to sleep and the missed requirements registering as a "zero" in the final score calculation.

Make your answers simple to find, read, and score, not an Easter egg hunt.

Which Style is Easier to Read and Score?

RFP Question:

Does your product include GIS mapping to an accuracy of 0.5 meters or less?

- Answer Example 1:

ABC Company's GIS mapping software has an accuracy rating of one foot measured over a 3-mile distance from .... (Buried in ten pages of the product description.)

- Answer Example 2:

Suppose each requirement is worth one point on the evaluator's scorecard. Let's assume each is a yes/no feature question out of 50, or 350. Read ten pages of narrative and look for the answers in the thickly written technical tea leaves like a scavenger hunt, or count the "yes" rows on a table. (And focus on any "no" responses?) Which style would you prefer to read and score?

RFP Requirement	ABC Company Complies	ABC Company Comments
Does your product include GIS mapping to an accuracy of 0.5 meters or less?	Yes	ABC Company's GIS mapping has an accuracy rating of one foot, approximately 0.32 meters.
Requirement 2	Yes	ABC Company exceeds requirement 2
Requirement 3	Yes	ABC Company exceeds requirement 3

Sample Requirements Table

Flexibility is Key

The rule to remember is to be flexible with your RFP response structure. While I prefer to use tables for their simplicity, if the directions state to copy each question into your response and answer each question separately, do it. Following RFP directions are my point about not relying on "boilerplate" content. I have seen such specifications, and I wouldn't say it is rare or frequent, more like 25-35% of cases.

We call being responsive to the requirements "answering the mail." If the RFP's instructions specify how to respond, you will not get any extra credit for ignoring that and doing your own thing. Instead, you could quickly be disqualified for being "non-responsive." More often than not, your RFP response will strongly resemble a regurgitation of the RFP solicitation, with your answers sprinkled in. I think all will agree that it is a boring document to read, but you can't go wrong with the approach either.

More complex approaches may combine the two. For example, if I am following a specification with dozens or hundreds of numbered paragraph headings for each "shall," "will," or "must" in the RFP. It starts to look pretty long, and I may use a very abbreviated version of the table above - such as a paraphrased requirement in the first column, a single "checkmark" in the second for the needs I meet, followed by a paragraph number where the requirement is discussed in the third column, hyperlinked to the start of the section.

RFP Requirement	ABC Company	Paragraph
GIS mapping to an accuracy of 0.5 meters or less?		

Sample Requirements Table with RFP Paragraph References

Brevity

The most common correlation for my wins and losses record is not using all of the "page budget" permitted by the RFP. If your page limit for a section is 50 pages, but you can answer everything in 25, feel free to ask any authority; you don't need to make up 50 pages of nonsense to make the document look bigger. No one awards points for paper tonnage.

Let's be honest with ourselves. These things are not action-packed epic novels to read. If you can keep it brief, by all means, do.

Pro Tip: If you can convey your offer in half of the maximum page count, resist the urge to fill out the rest with unneeded fluff. Sometimes less is more.

Submitting Questions

While developing requirements, I will also track "questions" that generate in my mind while reading the RFP in detail. A requirement's specifications or wording may not be precise, or other clerical errors in the RFP can lead to different conclusions, depending on the reader's interpretation. I will note my questions as I review the RFP, and sometimes another part of the RFP will clarify an ambiguity. I may also speculate my answer for other reasons. By tracking as I read through, I will generally have the most comprehensive understanding at the conclusion. If your proposal approach is dependent upon clarifications, you can submit your list of questions before the Q&A deadline indicated in the RFP. The agency will publicly respond to all of the questions it receives and their answers to all interested vendors. I don't look for "gotcha" questions here to point out clerical mistakes; I am only interested in obtaining answers to the ones that materially affect my approach or the pricing.

I wait until the Q&A deadline to submit because often, the same questions are asked by others. The agency may answer critical questions immediately. For example, RFP structural or timeline errors or inconsistencies are usually corrected quickly after discovery. There can be an advantage in not submitting questions if not necessary to do so. You are also not advertising your presence to competitors interested in the solicitation and are familiar with your company. When a rival is aware of your interest, their price may reflect that perception of increased competition, and they may bid lower than they may otherwise. The more competitors know about each other's interest in the opportunity, the lower the prices will likely be.

The best position to be in is having marketed your services to the agency well in advance during the Sources Sought and RFI phases, openly declaring your interest to the agency, having attended the workshops, and developing a solid understanding of the opportunity. In this case, you may intuitively know the answers to your questions and a broadcast of the intelligence to lesser-prepared competitors is not in your best interest. If you know quite a bit about the opportunity and are comfortable with your position, the "smarter" questions you may think about asking can help your competitors more than the answers will help you.

I will monitor the published Q&A, even if I didn't submit any questions myself. It's easy to identify the vendors "throwing some spaghetti on the wall to see if it sticks" because their questions are rudimentary or way off target.

My recommendation is if you feel like you are in a good position, only submit questions that you need an answer to for proposal content, technical requirement, or reasons that will affect your pricing, and only submit them just before the deadline (in case someone else asks the same question and you get the answer for free anyway).

Pro Tip: Often, agencies will not be able to post answers to the submitted questions by their posted deadline, when this the agency will usually extend the proposal submission deadline unilaterally. If not, an extension will be commonly granted if you need one.

Proposal Go / No-Go

If you have a lot of familiarity with your company, your products, or your services, this may be an optional step, depending on your industry, level of legal risk, the complexity of your product or service, staffing requirements, and other factors. I include this for businesses with a variable level of risk for each opportunity.

This step includes senior members of your organization engaged at a sufficient level for a final Bid or No-Bid decision. Sometimes a requirement of the opportunity may be a "no-go" for your company for reasons outside your area of expertise. For example, if it is a public works project and requires a $10 million bond with your final offer and your company is only bondable to $5 million, sorry, but you are not going to be building that new freeway overpass bridge (this time).

Other requirements can be show-stoppers. The opportunity may require specific types of insurance that you do not have and not be willing to procure (such as if the insurance upgrade cost is higher than your likely profit would be) or if you are organized as a sole proprietorship or partnership and organizational tax returns are required with the response. Is the company owner willing to provide their tax returns if necessary? Other internal questions can arise, and a quick review of your requirements spreadsheet with your proposal outline can uncover these before investing more of your time.

I suggest this step in your proposal process because of the reality of human nature. If you send 100+ page RFPs to the company's legal department, executives, and heads of business units to review when you receive them, few, if any, will read them. They have their job to do and are usually not interested in helping you with yours. I am not trying to insult anyone with this; don't construe this with any passive-aggressive intent. I have been in all of the roles, sales, marketing, business unit, and executive leadership. You will get much more participation if you break it down into a requirements spreadsheet and review critical requirements as a group in a one-hour web meeting. The daylight slips away from everyone, and it is usually more efficient to find an hour that everyone is available and work through it as a team. From experience, everyone else will appreciate the requirements spreadsheet "Cliffs Notes Version" instead of the 100-page RFP. If someone has questions about a specific need, the page and paragraph number in your location column make it a quick review during the same meeting, and when necessary, you can add it to your list of questions for Q&A submittal and reconvene when answers are received.

The Evaluation Process

Understanding how the prospective government customer will evaluate your offer can be very easy or difficult without much variation. Let me explain.

Many government solicitations will include an overview of how the evaluation team will score offers and how the winner(s) is selected. Sometimes the information provided may be quite detailed, such as each evaluation criterion and the maximum points available. Other times, there may only be some generalized information, such as "30% for past performance, 35% for technical proposal, and 35% for cost." Others do not indicate at all.

In my career, I have seen several different procurement competition types, some more often than others.

Lowest Price, Technically Acceptable (LPTA)

Having spent much of my career in technology products, I have encountered this procurement type more often than others. I prefer these, the evaluation strategy objective and well understood. To win, meet all of the specifications of the product or service sought at the lowest price among those deemed qualified - and you win. If no vendors are fully qualified, meaning all fall short in some way, the buyer may consider accepting the next best at the lowest price or canceling the procurement and redefining the specifications for another subsequent procurement attempt. In my experience, if the solicitation is an LPTA, the buying entity has a good understanding of the market and understands there may be minor variations of products between competitors with similar capabilities.

Best Value

Best Value procurements, also known as "tradeoff" evaluations in some jurisdictions, are commonly found in services solicitations, but

I have seen the strategy used for other procurements. These can be the most difficult to predict or win because evaluating the proposals received will be subjective. By definition, the government buyer will "prefer" the option that is the most advantageous to the government and not necessarily at the lowest price or the highest-quality product or service. Because of this open-ended sliding scale nature, I cannot offer much advice other than to mention my strategy.

If you know the customer, the business purpose, and the needs, then, by all means, use that to your advantage and offer what you believe the customer wants.

My strategy to win these when my knowledge of the customer is somewhat limited is pretty straightforward, with several variations by circumstance. First, if the need is well-within my "wheelhouse," meaning that I am a low-cost leader or brand name value-leader in the space, I'll meet the requirements "exactly." I may also throw in some extras if it doesn't cost anything, and then I'll go to the floor for what I would accept for a price and still be worth performing the contract. In other words, I'll treat it a lot like an LPTA purchase.

Sole Source

Sole source procurements are events triggered by a direct sale effort by the intended supplier. For example, Google is the only vendor of Google Workspace[1], and Microsoft is the sole provider of Office 365[2]. Other sellers exist, but those are resellers of the same product. For a large procurement, the government agency may desire to deal directly. Other common uses will be acquiring innovative technologies for which only a single provider exists.

Many sole sources are more "self-serving" than indeed a sole source. For example, many sole-source procurements for various technologies are perceived (by the buyer) to be unique and only available from a single provider - and the provider's competitors may disagree. I have worked in a field where this situation is familiar. Sole source procurements are commonly advertised in advance, usually allowing for a week for other offers to come forward. For these events, I will often write a kind letter notifying the buyer that other products are available for competitive solicitation. Sometimes the buyer will respond by asking for a demonstration; sometimes, there is no response, and a new solicitation is posted periodically.

Lowest price

Perhaps a mythical belief is that companies that do not engage with the government will most commonly perceive government contracting as "lowest-bidder." Rarely is this the case; the most common for the desired lowest price contract will be an LPTA. The military provides "MILSPEC" grade and material quality standards if buying bolts and rivets for jet fighter repair. LPTA stresses the only offers considered will be those that meet the published MILSPEC. We don't want a low-quality household-grade machine screw used in place of high-strength ultra-light aviation hardware. For road construction, concrete is not "concrete" - there are many grades of concrete - fast setting/high strength, high-strength, fast-setting (but not high strength), etc. There is even recycled concrete - and it doesn't hold up to semi-truck loads passing over it. For situations where the safety of life or war-fighting readiness is at risk, we want the government to buy only from vendors that meet the minimum specifications. For copier paper or paper clips, the lowest-price offer is probably satisfactory.

Other Transaction Authority

I have only encountered procurements via OTA from defense and national security customers. The definition of OTA is complex, and if you work in these markets, I recommend you separately research the concepts thoroughly - via any Internet search engine. These agencies have some capability to quietly purchase what they need from their suppliers without advertising their intent to do so. In short, the contractor provides an offer of the unique or innovative technology or solution, sort of as an unsolicited proposal, and the government reviews and discusses further, if interested.

Oral Interviews

Oral interviews are standard in the professional services, information technology, and construction industries but may not be for other fields. Smaller procurements will almost invariably skip this phase and award the contract to the most-qualified offer evaluated.

For the ones that include an oral interview phase, the agency will only offer the interviews to the most qualified offers following the evaluation phase. Offers deemed non-compliant, disqualified, or scored poorly on the technical or cost review will probably not advance to this phase.

The number of vendors selected for oral interviews can vary widely, but in my experience, only the top two, three, or four candidates are invited to participate.

My preparation for oral interviews depends on the potential contract size. Our typical/average sales size will be a presentation created by customizing one of our standard pre-canned presentations, and I'll do a few rehearsals in front of my webcam for the overall length. The customization to the presentation will be for areas of interest by the customer or specific questions that I expect. I do these presentations often, so it's an area of natural comfort for me. Others may need additional preparation.

Larger multi-year, high-value opportunities are different. These will involve a presentation crafted directly from our RFP response while incorporating our professional graphics team, and I'll likely do several days of rehearsal - sometimes with a professional presentation coach. These are worthy measures to consider if you are in the final two on a sale worth millions of dollars. The potential profit from the deal needs to justify the $2,500, $5,000, or $10,000 this may cost, but I highly recommend presentation coaches. I have never lost an opportunity when I have used one.

The format of oral interviews will vary, but for the most part, their goal is the same. They are looking for professionalism in the contractor, a cultural fit for their organization, and "can we work with this company?" Be professional, be personable, and listen more than you speak.

Commonly, you will be allotted a specified period. I design the presentation to consume ⅔ to ¾ of the time provided and reserve the remainder for questions and answers from the attendees.

Most importantly, try to be yourself. Give the process the respect it deserves, don't walk in wearing jeans and a polo shirt, and instead look like the company that wants to be a government contractor. I wear a sport coat and tie or a suit, depending on the weather and travel required. At a minimum, this is a shirt & tie for men and the equivalent for women.

Pro Tip: Oral interview coaches can be invaluable for the preparation of a major contract presentation.

Best and Final Offer (BAFO)

Best and Final Offers, or a BAFO, are sometimes requested from the final vendors under consideration after all other phases of offer evaluation. If you have been asked for a BAFO, you are likely within the only two or three vendors remaining under consideration.

Putting it straight, this is where you sharpen your pencil. If I know the remaining competitors through good intelligence, I will pull any recent public sector awards they may have to look at whatever may be contained. Their contract price will always be there, but the scope of work can sometimes be unknown. For example, one of my competitors likes to bid on their job with a quotation sheet, and it is frequently attached to the agency's award when published. Because of this, I can usually see their current pricing model as long as the services sold are sufficiently similar. I have included an overview of how to do this in Chapter 7, Competition.

Some vendors will intentionally leave a little room in their initial proposal to enable a more-aggressive BAFO phase. I can't speak to the merits of that, but I have done so myself occasionally. Research your competition ahead of time and go in with your comfortable pricing. Often you will learn more about the opportunity through the orals or feedback received from the contracting officer, and you can adjust your scope and pricing accordingly here.

Pro Tip: Be prepared with some room to additionally discount during a Best and Final Offer phase, doing so displays a strong interest in the contract.

Pro Tip: Best and Final Offers are not always requested. Leave some room in your proposal to present a BAFO if asked; but always price your proposal to win without a BAFO phase.

Award

A contract award is usually an exciting event. First, you won, so there is that - congratulations. But most importantly, when you consider the typical length of a procurement cycle - weeks, months, or even years - getting that email or phone call will always come when you are least expecting it and "really makes your day."

The style of notification will vary. If you have a good relationship with the customer, they will likely call you and email the news and contract to you. In other cases, you may get an email directing you to a web posting of the outcome.

Please pay attention to what you receive, and read it carefully to ensure it accurately represents your offer. Note, in almost all cases; your proposal is incorporated into the award by reference, even if it is not embedded in the document itself, so assume your contract to include the terms and conditions stated in the RFP, external documents incorporated by reference in the RFP, the content of your proposal, and any additional terms and conditions included.

Again, I do not dispense legal advice. If you usually have an attorney review your commercial contracts, you would certainly want one to review a public sector award. Be sure it is one familiar with government contracting.

After the award is sent to the prevailing vendor and the contract is returned to the agency with a signature executing the agreement, the contracting officer notifies the losing vendors. Vendors not selected are usually offered a debrief or can always request one.

Companies new to government contracting should always take the debriefing. Here the contracting officer will go over how the evaluation team scored your offer, your areas of strength, and your areas of weakness. Use this information to better your capabilities and approach proposal development to be more competitive on your next attempt.

Everyone else should take the debrief too, and the reason is the potential for protest.

Protests

One of the profound differences between the public sector and commercial sales markets is the ability to "protest" a public procurement award.

You have carefully followed the opportunity, reviewed the RFP when it was published, developed a strong proposal, priced it well, and did great in the oral interviews, but you still didn't win. Why? Who knows?

There may also be times when you disagree with the findings presented in your debrief. For example, maybe your proposal was quoted as an "annual" cost of service, and they incorrectly evaluated it as a "monthly." Maybe there was some unusually close "chummi-ness" between members of the evaluation panel and the company that prevailed, and you felt that the agency was only going through the legal motions while wasting everyone else's time. Some states and counties seem to have invented and still practice the concept of "cor-ruption." The US political process is certainly not as pure as the driven snow.

What can you do? You can file a protest if you think you have a good case and can cite specific examples where you were not treated as somewhat as you should have been. The instructions are generally provided within the RFP, published by the agency on their website, or sometimes included in your "Dear John" letter notifying you of your loss.

A protest formally escalates the award to a second-level review, often including the agency's legal team or an inspector general. They will review the scoring of the offers received, the pricing, and how each offer scorecard was calculated and ensure that linear approaches to scoring each criterion were used.

Why would you want to do this? For example, I have lost by 0.25 points before out of a 1,000-point evaluation. The winner was an incumbent doing business with the agency for over a decade, and I was the newbie. If I can get that close, the evaluation team may have used something arbitrary in the scoring that manifested as putting the finger on the scale.

Whatever your situation, you should not do this lightly. If you want a future relationship with the agency, arbitrarily filing a protest is not a great way to make friends or gain influence. However, if you think you have been wronged and have one or more specific examples, it's not a bad idea to try. I've won on a protest before, and I've only been involved in a few (less than 5).

Protests are widespread in certain types of contracts, large GWAC competitions where the agency will select many vendors from many offers, and large military procurements, for example.

Pro Tip: Filing protests is not the to make friends or gain influence, reserve them for when you strongly feel your proposal was overlooked.

---

1. Google Docs (Google Workspace) [Computer Software]. https://www.google.com/docs/about/.
2. Microsoft Office (Microsoft Office 365) [Computer Software]. https://www.microsoft.com/en-us/microsoft-365.

PART III

BUILDING A PUBLIC SECTOR BUSINESS STRATEGY

6

BUILDING A PUBLIC SECTOR BUSINESS DEVELOPMENT TEAM

Government business development teams require skills that differ from their commercial market counterparts, and market expectations for compensation plans will vary.

To plan your team, visualize the sales process we discussed in the previous chapter and what skills will be needed along the way. Does your commercial market sales team think strategically, such as planning today for opportunities that will not materialize into a biddable solicitation for 12 or 18 months? Is the sales team accustomed to drafting detailed documents that adhere to specific requirements or specifications? Are they comfortable competing against rivals while pricing firm-fixed contracts for multi-year contracts?

The good news is that many of these skills will already be in your company. The bad news is it probably isn't in your commercial sales team.

Commercial vs. Government Sales Teams

There are several reasons that most government contractors that do business with private and public sector customers will choose to separate their government and commercial sales team.

The technical differences between commercial and public sector sales practices and the length of the sales cycle itself are challenging to reconcile such an appraisal of the performance of a commercial versus a public sector salesperson with the same performance indicators would be inaccurate. Often, commercial sales teams are commission-driven, and standard measurements point to opening new opportunities and closing contracts in the same week/month/quarter, etc. The cycle from initial contact to signing a contract award can be many months or years in the public sector. How good the salesperson is will not matter if the project is not funded or anticipated until three years from now.

Considerations for Designing the Government Sales Team

Getting back to the design of the business development team, consider the phases of the government sales process that we discussed in the previous chapters. Initial contact, responding to a request for information, vendor days, marketing presentations, developing proposal responses to a formal request for proposal, working with partners, negotiating an award, teaming agreements, cooperative contracts, and frequently the need to establish and maintain relationships with individuals unrelated to the decision-making process, but critical to winning the award.

First, sharpen the tip of your marketing spear. Identify the best person in your company to communicate the availability of your product or services to the government sector. Invariably, these sales cycles will be pretty long, and you don't want to swap out your "single point of contact" regularly.

Second, responding to an RFI or RFP will require technical knowledge of your product or services and industry knowledge of warranty or support expectations in the marketplace, competitors, and how your products or services compare to others. Usually, the most qualified person for this will be a product manager, program manager, service delivery manager, or the equivalent for your industry.

Third, the necessary minimum quality of writing skills to draft the formal response documents. Of the various skills, this will usually be the most difficult one to fill. Unfortunately, writing doesn't seem to be a primary focus of the American public educational system anymore. Consider the resumes you receive for vacancies; how many have obvious spelling or grammar issues that tapping the "spellcheck button" would have probably fixed? How many are boring to read, badly organized, or poorly written? Are they five pages long when it seems like one or two would do? Is the person applying for a senior management position that requires 15 years of professional experience, but the resume starts with where they went to high school? How did the cover letter read? Did the person write a cover letter? If not, transmittals and executive summaries every week will be a challenge. These are examples of deficiencies that will find their way into formal sales documents, damaging the quality of the sales message.

Fourth, government agencies usually are awash in contractual terms, referenced external documents, policy papers, and regulations. To do this, you will need someone on the team comfortable with reading, analyzing, and enumerating the terms of the agreement for everyone to review. A lot of legal support is one option, or trusting the analytical judgment of the non-lawyers on the team is another.

Fifth, most contracts I compete for require an oral interviews phase. If you are in a similar industry, your team must excel at 30-minute technical presentations, 60-minute product demonstrations, and 30-minutes of questions and answers from a senior-level audience. The person that sweats through their pants onto the conference room chair during a job interview is not the person that will do well presenting to an evaluation panel of 5, 10, or 20 people.

Sixth, after winning your public sector contract, you will need someone allocated to executing your contractual responsibilities, protecting your interests, and serving as the point of contact for your public sector customer(s). Government agencies are large customers and are used to having a high level of service, no matter how minor the contract may be. Besides, doing an excellent job on the small ones will serve as references to get the bigger ones. A solid customer-facing resource here can also be a vital member of the government sales team.

Compensation Plans for Government Sales

Some types of government procurement produce regular and recurring orders and revenue, such as an inside sales representative for an office supplies company that receives weekly orders. For most, though, the sales efforts will focus on fewer but larger projects or sales contracts. Most of the time, your team will need a reasonable base salary combined with a revenue-based (commission) bonus plan.

Government Sales Team Organization

I have had the fortune to work with several employers and clients for over twenty years, and I have seen several approaches to organizing a government business development team.

The first, and usually the most effective for professional service companies, is to allocate sales resources to a small area, such as a specific state government or agency. Focusing on a single market grows relationships with prospective customers and accumulates market intelligence about upcoming opportunities. This approach is more expensive in terms of sales staff cost but will produce the best results. An obvious variable is what your business is selling and the level of market interest in a particular agency or region for it.

The second is to allocate sales staff by product or service expertise, but not limited by geography. For example, the sales rep or sales team only focuses on the company's data warehousing product but will follow sales leads in any geographic location. For technical products, particularly with a small customer base, the advantages of this approach are lower cost while grooming a specialized sales team, messaging, and pricing strategy.

The third approach is a minor sales team that offers all or most of the company's products and services to any region or market. Often the lack of specialization in a specific product or market will result in lower opportunity close rates. Variables are the company's market and product competitiveness and existing market share or brand recognition. In essence, this approach is a numbers game. The proposal tempo from the US's thousands of public sector markets will limit the time available for opportunity research, proposal preparation, customer relationship building, and accumulating market and opportunity intelligence.

Getting Ahead of Your Competition

Your competitors are meeting with government agencies that may be interested in your products or services well ahead of any procurement activities, so you should be too. Another less-obvious advantage is if the agency is not interested or is happy with their existing long-term contract, you can plan for an aggressive pricing offer or cross it off your list and focus your attention elsewhere.

Your approach to getting a meeting scheduled on the agency's calendar will vary, and there isn't a single best answer for all situations. The most prominent strategies are usually the most effective.

First, I recommend calling or emailing the contracting officer, if known and asking for a meeting. If they respond, they will likely ask who else you would like to present, which should be the relevant business managers for the program or opportunity of interest.

Second, although less effective, in my opinion, you can try using social media professional networking sites, although anecdotally, I would estimate far less than half of your target contacts will have a social media profile.

And last, with more of a luck factor than a skill, trade show booths or attendance will put you in proximity to the people who may be interested in your product or service. Whether the one you are looking for is there will, of course, be a luck factor. I usually attend several trade shows annually to increase my professional network and relationships, and these will usually spin off a large dividend later when you least expect it.

If you are in a hurry to build some marketing contacts, buy a booth at an upcoming public sector industry conference for something relevant to what you do. Spend some time researching the groups, sponsors, and attendees; a great sign is if you see your competitors attend the same ones you are studying.

Playing a Long Game

To get a meeting, be realistic. Do some research and identify the likely "buyers" for the agency and business units that may be interested in what it is you are offering. Organizational charts and staff directories are helpful for this, and often you can find one online with just a Google search. Conduct some research, find a likely office unit, look up their procurement or contracting office, and there will generally be an info@ or other general information contact email address and phone number. Don't be discouraged if no one picks up your call; leave a message with what you are asking for (a meeting), and someone will generally call you back. I recommend you start with a meeting request for "process" and ask for a referral to the best-suited individuals in their organization. Most of them will oblige. I begin by introducing myself and asking for their help.

Other avenues everyone will probably try are emailing the agency director, connecting on LinkedIn, and the electronic messaging equivalent of cold-calling. These strategies have never worked for me, and I don't recommend them, but I am certainly not the cold-calling type either.

The Short Cut

Industry conferences and similar events work very well. Do you make a sale there? If you do, you are better than I am! However, I make a lot of contacts and a lot of friendships. For example, I attend a yearly trade show that guarantees meetings with at least a half-dozen state procurement chiefs or similar positions. I get fifteen minutes, one-on-one, to make my pitch, and I get a referral to other agencies and specific individuals with resources and potential interests. My secret is I make the pitch in about 7 or 8 minutes and spend the other half of the time asking my new contact how the show has been going, how their year has been at work and getting to know them. Inevitably I run into them later in the show at one of the social events and take a more ample opportunity to develop the relationship. On a good year, the two days at the conference will turn into eight or nine new good leads from different states across the country.

Follow-ups

Follow-ups are the area where I shine. I have a lot of personal history and places of interest. I am a service-disabled veteran on an ice curling team, I have had several businesses, my wife and I travel a lot with our RV, and I have tried every quirky activity from skydiving to gold panning to metal detecting and my newest fascination with my eBike. These experiences give me potential areas of common ground with almost anyone I meet, and I just "be myself," what you see is what you get, and it works for me. Are you more inclined to pick up the phone or answer the doorbell for a neighbor you have had (and have liked) for a decade or the vacuum cleaner salesperson that is only interested in trying to go as fast as they can to get to a "yes"? I rest my case.

I do find that I "gravitate" more toward customers that have these similar interests or backgrounds, and instead of just being a customer - they usually end up as new lifelong friends as well. I am sure the other vendors that call are happy to bore them with the latest version of XYZ software they are selling. Instead, I'm the guy that talked about camping on the beach in Corpus Christi last month. The other vendors might have cell phone numbers, but I know their kids' names, what their spouse does for a living, where they like to go on vacation, the bourbon they want to try, and other details that only their friends know.

Is this a selling tactic? Not really; instead, it's not intentional; it's just the person I am. It's also the only way I know how to sell - I'm not a salesperson; I have been a business consultant of some flavor for over 20 years, so it is what works for me.

Small Business Certification Programs

Small businesses have certain advantages over larger companies concerning government contracting. The US Small Business Administration (SBA)[1], under the authority granted to it within the Small Business Act, has established programs to help firms owned or controlled by socially and economically disadvantaged individuals.

One program is not necessarily better than another; each has its eligibility requirements. Awards are not necessarily in "competition" between these groups; each will have its own pool of set-aside opportunities. A set-aside is an opportunity for which only certification members can compete. For example, an opportunity may be limited to only "Minority-Owned Small Businesses" or "Woman-Owned Businesses."

Any small business serious about building a government contracting business should apply for and obtain the best-relevant program with an eligibility match.

Small Business

The most basic category is that of a "Small Business." This designation is self-certified by stipulating your business meets the requirements for the NAICs code being used for the solicitation. Usually, this will be a gross revenue maximum or a limit on the number of employees in your company. It varies by industry. The SBA has a table of size standards by NAIC code on its website. Small business benefits are minimal, usually in the form of a slight price advantage. The government also provides a limited number of small business set-aside opportunities.

Eligibility

- Open to everyone with US citizenship
- Income or Company Size Limits by NAICs Code

Veteran-Owned Small Business (VOSB)

Known as Vets First, the US Department of Veterans Affairs manages the VOSB program and makes available set-aside and sole-source contracts for requirements solicited by the VA. Some other federal agencies also utilize the VOSB program, notably the Department of Defense, and many states have similar programs at the state level. There is no minimum set-aside target for contracting awards to VOSBs.

Eligibility

- The Veteran business owner must have previously served on Active Duty in the Army, Air Force, Marine Corps, Navy, or Coast Guard at any time.
- The Veteran must have been discharged under conditions other than "dishonorable."
- Reservists and National Guard members are eligible if they have been called to Federal Active Duty at any time.
- The Veteran must own at least 51% of the business.
- The Veteran must have complete control over the business operations.
- The business must be a small business per the SBA's size standards for the NAICs Code.

Service-Disabled Veteran Owned Small Business (SDVOSB)

Similar to the VOSB, the SDVOSB program is an additional set-aside program operated by the VA. SDVOSB program participants can also participate in the VOSB program, but the SDVOSB has different eligibility requirements. SDVOSB set-asides are limited to only SDVOSB-certified participants. SDVOSBs may self-certify their status for most federal agencies, but the VA will only recognize a VA-certified program participant.

Eligibility

- Be at least 51% owned and controlled by one or more service-disabled Veterans.
- Have one or more service-disabled Veterans manage day-to-day operations and also make long-term decisions
- The controlling Veteran must also have a service-connected disability with a disability rating of 0% to 100% (no minimum).
- The business must be a small business per the SBA's size standards for the NAICs Code.

Woman-Owned Small Business (WOSB)

The federal government has a goal of 5% of all federal contracting dollars being awarded to woman-owned small businesses annually.

There is an Economically Disadvantaged Woman Owned Small Business Program (EDWOSB), but it has requirements aligned to the 8(a) program below. Certify as an 8(a) instead of the EDWOSB; the 8(a) program is substantially more valuable.

Eligibility

- Be at least 51% owned and controlled by women that are also US citizens.
- Women manage day-to-day operations and make long-term decisions.
- The business must be a small business per the SBA's size standards for the NAICs Code.

8(a) Business Development Program

The 8(a) program is a nine-year program designed to grow small businesses into larger functioning companies. Participating firms receive training and technical assistance designed to strengthen their ability to compete in the US economy. Federal agencies partner with the SBA to promote the maximum utilization of 8(a) program participants. Certified firms can efficiently compete for set-aside and sole-source federal contracts and will receive one-on-one business development assistance from an SBA Business Opportunity Specialist. The SBA also offers a Mentor-Protege program, partnering new 8(a) program participants with graduated, successful companies. Many Mentor-Protege partners will form a Joint Venture, increasing their capacity to bid on much larger projects than the 8(a) could perform independently.

Eligibility

- Be a small business, as designated by the NAIC Code.
- Not have previously participated in the 8(a) program.
- Have a personal net worth of less than $750,000 or less, an adjusted gross income of $350,000 or less, and assets totaling $6 million or less.
- Demonstrate good moral character (no criminal convictions)
- Demonstrate the potential for success by having been in business for at least two years before program application

*Note, tribal-owned companies, Alaskan Native corporations, Community Development Corporations, and Native Hawaiian companies can always apply for and maintain 8(a) program certification without income, size, or asset limits and will not sunset out of the program after nine years.

Other Than Small (OTS)

Only mentioning to define it for the reader. Companies other than small businesses (medium or large, for example) are not small businesses and are regarded as "other than small" by the federal government. There are no associated set-aside programs.

First Win Targets

Housing authorities prefer business owners that are currently or were recently former tenants [of the government housing programs]. If you are starting on your public sector sales efforts and you are currently or have recently received housing subsidies, I highly recommend you look into contracting solicitations from the housing authority in your city. You may be standing in a short line for some fantastic opportunities.

Transit authorities are locally operated but heavily funded by the federal government, and their procurement decisions are influenced by conditions attached to the federal funding. These conditions are often in the form of socioeconomic set-aside provisions and preferences. If your firm has relevant designations, you should prominently mention those in your RFI response for state or local agencies using federal funds.

Unemployment agencies have similar federal grant funds as those mentioned above but operate more independently in my observation and experience.) Set-asides, anecdotally, seem more like a "guideline" than a rule for these agencies, but my information is only from personal observation.

---

1. SBA Federal Contracting Assistance Programs. (2022). https://www.sba.gov/federal-contracting/contracting-assistance-programs.

PART IV

PLANNING TO WIN

7

PLANNING TO WIN

I f you want to win, plan to do so.

Government procurement is a long game; if you plan to meet your monthly sales goal next week, this isn't the market for you.

Marketing

Before any procurement effort begins, market your products or services to the prospective customer. Request a meeting to discuss your firm's capabilities and advantages, and provide a presentation and demonstrations. Ask questions, solicit feedback from the participants, and take the time to know and understand their needs.

Sources Sought and Requests for Information (RFI)

Sources sought, and RFI responses are the easiest way to create new connections with an agency interested in procuring the types of goods or services you offer. Many contracting friends will say, "It's only an RFI," and skip making the early phase efforts. I use RFIs to get my foot in the door, which has led to big opportunities several times. Remember, once the RFP is published, the only information you will receive that you do not already have, is the RFP content, any research you may be able to find, and published question & answer clarifications provided to everyone.

Opportunity Intelligence

Opportunity intelligence is critical. If the incumbent's award was part of another scope of work or issued as a task order on a GWAC, the information may not be readily findable with commonly used tools. I will research the agency's contracts before the solicitation. If I do not find what I am looking for ahead of time, it is perfectly acceptable to ask during the Q&A. The request for the incumbent's name and contract number is a commonly submitted question.

Under the Freedom of Information Act (FOIA), the incumbent's proposal, award, and the contract is public record, but in my experience, getting a response to a FOIA request is a "seldom" situation. I have several requests outstanding as of this writing for a competitor's contracts with a federal agency submitted at least two years ago, and I regularly get an update, "we are still working on your request." While you have a right to obtain a copy, unless you are prepared to file a civil action against the agency, you will probably not receive it in time to be of use.

Market Intelligence

Investing considerable time into researching competitors' other offers in the public sector market can be worthwhile. You can look for your competitors' contracts with other states or agencies if you sell products or services in a national or multi-state market. Be sure to pay attention to the dates of those contracts, mainly if your industry has seen prices rise or fall over the years. By obtaining a few samples, you may be able to understand and predict their pricing.

The stability and regularity of payments, larger order sizes, and multi-year contracts draw a lot of interest from competitors that you may not run into in the local B2B market. You may even find "new" competitors that have never heard of operating in the government space. These may be "box shops" or "check cashers" instead of companies with similar capabilities to yours. Small businesses with limited resources can have a socioeconomic certification advantage and act as resellers or prime contractors for larger companies. The large companies provide the product or services, but the small business brings the disadvantaged small business certifications of whatever type and the contracting preference. There are rules around the minimum work share that a small business prime must contribute, but for smaller-sized contracts, it is legal for them to subcontract 100% of the effort to a larger company.

I will also look for competitors' recent wins in the same region or customer type for clues as to where the competitive price range may be.

Pro Tip: Opportunity intelligence is the most important resource you can acquire.

Understanding Competition

I use a tactic to attend the bidders' conference whenever offered potential opportunities. I rarely learn anything of value, but I am not there to listen to the instructions on how to read an RFP. I am there for two other reasons.

First, I listen to the questions others ask to gauge the level of market knowledge and technical expertise among the competitors. I avoid asking questions unless there is something important on my mind because I don't want my question or the answer to help a marginally qualified competitor. I will limit the only questions I ask to confusion regarding the RFP's stated requirements, conflicting statements, conflicting due dates, or extensions.

Second, I'll put on my corporate espionage hat and snap a picture of the sign-in sheet. All public contracts are public records, and you can request copies of the guest list, but time is usually going to be of the essence, and it is easier to have the information on hand. I intentionally arrive close to the start time or hang out in the lobby, trying to be near the last to sign in.

The attendee list becomes my research index. I can quickly determine which companies were present, what each one sells or provides, their price ranges on previous contracts, their strengths, and any perceived vulnerabilities. Unlike the B2B commercial market, where your offer is often the only one or one of a small number of offers being considered, government contracts will usually attract several to dozens of proposals. You not only have to sell your concept or solution to the decision-makers, but you also have to show that you are the best option among many offers.

Teaming

Small and disadvantaged businesses may have a socioeconomic "set-aside" or scoring advantage (and preference) compared to other offers. Only bidders with the designated socioeconomic certification can submit a proposal if the opportunity is specified as a set aside.

You can play that game too. If you qualify for a disadvantaged contractor program, obtaining your certification should be very high on your list of things to do. If you don't qualify, look for partners in your market or region and proactively ask for a meeting to gauge their level of interest and determine where your business goals align. A small firm that is successful and active in government contracting will usually "always" be interested in discussing opportunities with new teaming partners. Even if they already have one or more that they work with, having additional ones that can provide people and equipment or other resources will broaden the scale of their operation.

Usually, common interests among teaming partners will align to something like both parties making more money, but there are other strategic interests for both. For the software industry, I look for companies that provide complimentary technologies or supportive services to what I am offering. Providing on-site consulting services, product training, or software integration is always of interest for revenue and profit reasons to do "in-house," but it also doesn't scale as well as selling software. For scalability, it is hard to beat the outsourcing strategy, but it is also more challenging to maintain a consistent level of service quality.

Scaling Services with Partners

If I were to win "x" (fill in the blank) new customers in the same month, for the sake of argument, I hit it out of the park with five proposals last month, and all five sent award letters the following month, and they want to begin their contracts within two weeks. That is five new customer onboarding, service customizations, and a series of training classes for hundreds of people (at each customer) and all with the same deadline. Those are also "y" number of new opportunities to work in parallel, follow up on, and track while working on the new basket of contract awards.

If I have two small business partners available, I may elect to pay the subcontractors to provide the software training for the two most minor new awards while my in-house resources focus on the three most important ones and the "y" new proposals going out in the next few weeks.

If incorporating the small business subcontractors into the original proposal and pricing, I may be able to claim small business participation preference, and the customer will be able to consider the local community impact on their purchase decision. The small business subcontractor also counts toward any quotas I must meet on the cooperative contract vehicle if one was used.

Meanwhile, I'll focus internal resources on the tasks and services unique to our product knowledge capabilities.

The same argument applies to almost any industry involving people, transportation, or manufacturing. There is always a finite amount of capacity available within the company, and taking on permanent new hires for what may be a temporary situation is never wise. When necessary, sign the agreement with the subcontractor, get through implementation, and move on to the next one. As they say, it is always "better to make a small part of something instead of 100% of nothing;" with the government, the opportunity will almost always lead to other future business.

An often overlooked benefit of small business subcontracting is the potential for a fantastic quality of capabilities, staffing, customer knowledge, and resourcefulness of the small firms.

Picking a Teammate

Selecting a teaming partner is where the challenging work is. Do your research, and find the ones that already have some knowledge of the customer or an ongoing business relationship. From those, look at technical alignment with your area of expertise, and make sure they are not already doing business with your competitors. Above all, only pick the ones with a lot of experience in public sector selling. You don't want to waste the resources and opportunity cost by conducting a lot of on-the-job training. There are lots of options out there. Pick the ones that enhance your company's offer, not those that may detract from it.

When there are several potential partners to pick from, it is entirely acceptable to send out a survey and ask them to complete it. I use a simple spreadsheet for this, and I'll create a list of the capabilities that I am interested in going down in one column, and across the top row, I'll add a variety of agencies I am targeting. If I am researching for a specific opportunity, I'll still throw some other random agencies across the top to avoid disclosing my plan. I'll ask each potential partner to fill out the matrix with a self-scoring of 0-5, 0 indicating they have "zero experience" providing that service to that agency, and a "5," meaning they are doing so currently (for that customer). A "4" is currently performing that service for another agency. A "2" is something they have done in the past but not presently performing. Proposal scoring is usually weighted toward past performance references, so tallying how each prospective subcontractor can contribute to your win is an essential strategic practice. Before doing so verify if prime contractors can use subcontractors' references in proposal submissions. If the RFP doesn't specify, submit the question during the Q&A phase.

Services Performed	Agency "A"	Agency "B"
Software Training	3	5
User Account On-Boarding	3	5
Security Configuration	3	5

Sample Subcontractor Evaluation Scorecard

Services Performed

Using the example shown above, the prospective teammate would be of more value when selected for a proposal presented to "Agency B," while dropping to a second choice for "Agency A" if a more appropriate option is available and willing.

Joint Ventures

Joint ventures are formal legal entities between two or more businesses. The intent is to operate as a separate company or brand, as a proxy, while each retains its own identity and independent company.

I can identify pros and cons, but overall, I am not a fan because of the added complexity, tax filings, insurance policies, and the need to either formally dissolve it or continue operating it after the completion of the contract. I don't fault advocates for these, but they are not for me.

Are You the Small Business?

Now let's flip this around. What if you are a small business? How do you "max out" the selection points in the table above?

As a small business interested in being a subcontractor to a larger company on larger contracts, "check the boxes." First, any certifications your company may be eligible for should be your priority. Whether that is simply an SBA-certified small business or if upgrades are available to you, such as a woman-owned small business, service-disabled veteran-owned small business, or a disadvantaged small business in the form of an 8(a) or HubZone designation. If you qualify for more than one, get all of them.

Pro Tip: Teaming opportunities bring participation in larger contracts and normally equals more money.

Pro Tip: Teaming can add resources and references to your proposal to put it over the top during the evaluation phase.

Subcontracting Plans

I am a big fan of subcontracting but am not fond of subcontracting plans. That said, my view is limited to the small and medium-sized companies I specialize in, so I'll stick to the basics.

For service sector industries, public works projects, and research and development, the prime contractors may require many subcontractors, and the subtle nudging by the government to spread the wealth around makes a lot of sense. For others, like product companies that ship or sell a finished product, finding a need for any subcontracting becomes pretty challenging. It quickly becomes the exercise of trying to find a job for each of several with different backgrounds.

Fortunately, subcontracting plans are submitted and negotiated as a goal, not a guarantee. I usually submit with zero subcontracting goals met and zero across socioeconomic subcategories in my product world.

More recently, the US federal government has altered its subcontracting plan templates in favor of commercial product companies, adding a category for companies that sell products or services off the shelf. I had criticized the previous approach, and I am sure others had too, and fortunately, we now have a new category with a better fit for product sales.

My Criticisms

I don't want to turn this into a rant, but I also want to explain my position.

Let's suppose the government is trying to acquire software to do some basket of operations. One company is offering to build a custom piece of software for the government, with 25% sociodemographic subcontractor participation. The second company offers their off-the-shelf product that meets all requirements and does 50 other things for free.

In nearly every case, the custom-built software solution will be much more expensive to buy up-front and more costly to maintain over time. We have all heard the horror stories of states still using mainframes developed with COBOL programming language even while the very last of the COBOL programmers now qualifies for his or her senior citizen discount card. Some states keep dozens of developers for these systems on the payroll just in case something needs to be changed.

Option two, the vendor of the commercial off-the-shelf product, has made a substantial investment for research and development separately of selling for this unique opportunity, and let's assume there is pressure by its ownership to reach profitability soon. Naturally, there is a need to charge as much as the market will bear for their product, but it will be lower than a custom-developed solution, and the software maintenance is included in the licensing plan.

The vendor for option one anticipates a software development team of thirty-five, a couple of project managers, a half-dozen quality-control people, and a basket of software development-related subcomponent licensing, vacations and holidays, sick leave, and other related costs over two years. The custom solution becomes incredibly easy to find subcontracting opportunities; they may outsource the database server development portion, IT support, maintenance, quality control, and system testing. Maybe they subcontract portions of all o the above.

The vendor for option two has a couple of setup and integration tasks. They will be assigning user accounts and training the government's staff. Software companies do not subcontract their provisioning and security, so that the only option may be software training. To meet their subcontracting goals, they will need to identify software training firms, determine their ownership and socioeconomic structures, negotiate a price, and pay for the staff time from the prime vendor and the subcontractor to train the new trainers on the software and features. Hopefully, it is not a specialized product like law enforcement case management, government budget accounting software, or legal research libraries because the trainers will probably need a similar professional background to the audience to answer the typical work-related questions. One can quickly see how this becomes very expensive with uncertain outcomes.

My second criticism is the use of overly broad size standards. Anything over about $10 million at the state level or $32 million per year in the federal market is usually "large business" in the eyes of the government. A software company with something like $50 million of revenue will be grouped into the same "other-than-small" category as one with $50 billion annual revenue. Indeed, these are two different planes of existence, but both are given the same "other than small" handicaps.

What is a Subcontracting Plan?

When seeking a cooperative contracting contract with the federal government, such as a GSA Federal Supply System (FSS) schedule award, companies regarded as "other than small" must also submit their subcontracting plan with goals for each type of small business subcontractor. Examples include 8(a), Veteran-Owned Small Businesses, Service-Disabled Veteran-Owned Small Businesses, Woman-Owned Small Businesses, and Disadvantaged Small Businesses (minority-owned).

When required, the Subcontracting Plan is a blueprint for allocating resources (money) your firm will spend on various subcategories of small businesses. One might assume that some intelligence would go into these, such as if your business is located near a large native reservation with a significant federal contracting presence or you are in the defense industry. You have ready access to many veteran-owned businesses with specialties that you can use, and you should be able to allocate more of your resources toward specific, plentiful, local resources, right? That would be an incorrect assumption. In my experiences submitting and negotiating these, the only approach that seems to work is making each category an equal participant to the others.

On a quarterly or annual basis, as stated by the contract's reporting requirements, you will submit a statement documenting your subcontracting dollar volume for each project, or your company, for the reporting period.

Federal subcontracting plans allow the contractor to select an option to calculate the goal by project or company-wide for each reporting period. Speaking anecdotally, public works construction contractors would be much more in favor of reporting on a per-project basis, versus the software vendor may find it easier to report company-wide quarterly. I don't have an opinion on either. I suggest whatever would be the lesser burden to your company.

What Happens if you Don't Meet Your Goal?

If the company is making a good-faith effort to meet its goal, it is unlikely there will be any negative consequences. I have sometimes met my goals, but I have sometimes failed. I have tried on all of them. I recommend everyone take that approach.

The federal government defines a good faith effort in section 19.705-7 of the FAR. I can summarize a few things the contracting officer is directed to look for in determining if a good faith effort has been made.

Does the contractor break up its available work into pieces conducive to subcontractor participation?

It would be best if you considered a modular approach to your work. Instead of a subcontractor submitting one person to your team, subcontracting a specific function can be more of a fit for both. Construction companies do this all of the time. They subcontract the plumbing, framing, drywall, painting, or all of the above in different subcontractor bidding opportunities. They are not asking for a sub to contribute one framer, for example, to work with nine of their own.

Is the contractor actively looking for subcontractors to participate?

Some solicitations will provide a price preference for a targeted level of small subcontractor participation. For example, let's say the target is a 5% cost bonus. A 5% bonus means if contractor A bids $100,000 without a subcontractor, and contractor B submits $104,900 with a targeted subcontractor, contractor B is considered the lowest-priced bidder. That is not a typo. To make sense, the cost of using the subcontractor has to be within 5% of the overall project price versus the savings of using an internal resource. To prove this, I retain all of my research notes, I'll archive email conversations, and of course, the bids themselves.

Does the contractor solicit subcontracting participation early in the proposal process to provide subcontractors with adequate time to participate in the proposal and pricing?

Is the contractor negotiating with subcontractors in good faith?

Does the contractor direct small subcontractors to the SBA for needed assistance?

Financing a small business is a separate book and something I'll consider doing. These suggestions are from the FAR; they are not my own. They are written by people that perceive people that own or work for a small business as neanderthal cousins to large businesses' modern humans. For example, if the small subcontractor is undercapitalized, they can generally use a government contracting award as collateral for SBA financing. As a policy, I struggle with this, I would hesitate before recommending my subcontractor get an SBA line of credit, which would likely cross-collateralize his or her family home, vehicles, and savings, to help me meet my subcontractor goals.

Does the contractor assist the small subcontractor with lines of credit, bonding, insurance, equipment, supplies, or services? (Or do they send their subcontractors a copy of my book!?)

Humor aside, I recommend carefully researching suggestions made by the FAR separately. One of the tests for whether a resource is an employee or contractor will always be the requirement to supply their tools and supplies. The IRS defines this as one of the tests of an employee versus an independent contractor. If providing the FAR's suggestions of assistance to a subcontractor, the prime could find subject to IRS problems regarding what determines an "employee" versus a "contractor." Gaining a slight cost preference is not worth a future audit whacking your company for several years of unpaid payroll tax filings and late fees. Worse, your state may also investigate this, and the state won't care about your federal subcontractor plan goals.

Although failing to meet one subcontractor's socioeconomic goal, did the contractor exceed in another socioeconomic category?

This one is self-explanatory, and I think it is an excellent case. It is not reasonable to send your 8(a) home because you met your goal, and now you have to bring in a HubZone subcontractor, followed by a woman-owned next month. In practice, when I find a subcontractor I like, and they are performing well, I reward them with more business. I won't say, "Gee whiz, I'm sorry, you did great on that last contract, but you have the wrong skin color." Or, "You are doing great as a service-disabled veteran-owned small business, but the problem is, I am maxed out on handicapped subcontractor dollars; I need to find a veteran that is able-bodied." I can't imagine doing something like that, and I never will, but if you pay attention to the category requirements, that is what the socioeconomic distribution requires if taken at face value.

Not Attempting to Meet Your Goal

Not making an effort is more of a problem in government contracting. Above, we mentioned a few things that indicate that the contractor is making a good faith effort to meet its subcontracting goals. But what are some signs that the contractor has no intention of doing so? Again, the FAR directs contracting officers to investigate such a suspicion.

Failure to attempt to research and discover potential socioeconomic subcontractors.

If you do not look for subcontractors, you will probably never find one. Small businesses will usually be bootstrap funded by the owner's savings, credit, and family contributions. There is rarely room in the budget for a robust national marketing program. Take the time, make an effort, and do a little research using Sam.gov, Deltek GovWin IQ, or SBA directories, and you will find a lot of potential candidates for your program's goals.

Failing to designate and maintain a company official to administer the subcontracting program.

Designate a person of influence in your company to carry this out. It doesn't need to be their only job, and usually won't be, but you need to assign an advocate for your small business subcontracting program and incentivize them for each successful contribution to a winning proposal.

Failure to submit acceptable subcontracting plan reports.

The reports are due quarterly and annually. I'll admit, I sometimes [usually] miss the deadline on these, despite a gaggle of reminders in my calendars, and to-do apps make it happen. Some of the reporting systems are easy to use, and I am always on time with those. The federal government's approach is painful, and I tend to kick that can down the road sometimes. I think everyone gets some "love letters" in their inbox from time to time when they miss the due dates; it happens. Catch it up and move on.

Part of the problem, I think, is the lack of appreciation by government contracting officers of how many of these some of us file. I do business in all 50 states and the federal government, and I have a half-dozen cooperative contracts to manage. Conservatively, I do about 30 of these and similar reports every quarter. That is not enough to be a "job" for someone, but it is certainly enough that a few will fall through the crack during a busy end of a month.

There should be a subscription-based tracking app that acts as a one-stop clearing house for all of the forms a company files. Someone build one; I'll get you the contracts.

Adoption of company-wide processes or policies that would frustrate plan goals.

I'm sure some companies have done this, or it wouldn't be on the FAR's list, but I have never seen a company drop something like this in their policies manual.

Failure to pay the subcontractors.

Pay the subs if you hire them. Failure to pay the subcontractors is less of a program reporting issue and more of a breach of contract. Of course, as a prime contractor, you have a legitimate interest in safeguarding they have completed the work and it meets standards specified in your contract with the government and subcontracting agreements. If this isn't the problem, they need to be paid. Your subcontractors can also seek payment directly from the contracting officer if they have not been paid. That would make you look terrible.

Failure to correct substantiated findings in contractor reviews of the subcontracting program.

Having your program reviewed as you approach the last year of your cooperative contract or your underlying master agreement is not unusual. I have been through several of these, and I have missed some minor things that the contract required, which we immediately corrected. It is not a big deal. Quickly correct deficiencies and promptly notify the contracting officer accordingly.

Failure to provide the contracting officer with a written explanation if the contractor fails to acquire articles, equipment, supplies, services, or materials or perform construction work.

Obtain the work and supplies or services from your subs for your project. The problem will be self-correcting if someone doesn't perform for you.

Falsifying records of subcontract awards to small business concerns.

My recommendation, many documents you file will instruct "under penalty of perjury" somewhere on them. Your public sector customers can technically refer you to prosecution, which is not the desired outcome. File the truth, don't make something up, and don't sugarcoat a mistake. File as it is and notify the contracting officer immediately that you are taking corrective action.

Independent Contractor Regulations and Teaming Agreements

Earlier in this book, I mentioned how GSA's suggested "best practices" for subcontractor goal compliance will run afoul of state and federal independent contractor regulatory guidelines. As part of this risk mitigation chapter, I am revisiting and expanding.

Government contracting commonly involves contractor teaming agreements, joint ventures, prime and subcontractor arrangements, and supply chain relationships. I am an enthusiastic advocate for these arrangements for reasons I have mentioned elsewhere in the book.

Teaming agreements bring their own basket of risks, and the "prime" contractor (the one submitting the proposal) bears virtually all the risk and needs to be compensated for doing so. For example, when a prime contractor adds a subcontractor (or a supplier) to provide the services or products related to a specific portion of the scope of work if the subcontractor fails to perform or fails to provide the services or products committed to, the prime contractor is still obligated to do so for the government. Usually, this means finding another subcontractor.

We discussed the positive effects of contractor teaming in previous chapters. Now let's look at common risks to mitigate.

Teaming Agreements

The government likes teaming arrangements so much that it provides sample agreement templates with your favorite search engine. In general, I recommend the agreement includes the following:

1. Who does what concerning the proposal preparation?

2. What (if any) references will the subcontractor agree to provide to the proposal.

3. What roles, task orders, products, or labor types will the subcontractor provide. It is also a good idea to enumerate the prime contractor's roles and responsibilities, but it is assumed the prime will do "all others."

4. How will the prime compensate the subcontractor?

5. Any other necessary terms and conditions

Prime and Subcontractor Relationship Risks

The IRS provides several tests of an independent contractor versus employer-to-employee relationship:

1. Behavioral, does the prime contractor exert control over when the subcontractor shows up for work or how the work is done?

2. Financial, is the business aspects of the subcontractor controlled by the prime; these include specific compensation levels, expense reimbursements, and who buys any equipment or tools.

3. Operational, does the prime specify vacation time, sick leave, fringe benefits, or anything of that nature?

Opening a subcontractor relationship with a separate corporation with its own employees, benefits, and operating budget are much safer than the risk of working with a sole proprietorship. This is not to belittle entrepreneurs, which I have the utmost respect for.

The IRS's interest in "independent contractors" is whether self-employment or payroll taxes are paid. A separate established company with its own accounting system, employees, and payroll tax filings is minimal risk to the prime contractor. The challenge of an independent operator stems from any blurred lines, paying the subcontractor for vacation hours or buying their tools and computers. Don't do it.

Subcontractors should remit a periodic invoice specifying the work completed, hours of labor performed, or other measurements, and a due date for payment. The prime contractor can determine the type of people provided regarding skills, experience, and the security requirements mentioned earlier, but not the "who."

Intelligence Tools

The government sales team will require a variety of tools that are unique to our industry. Mostly, these are freely available or subscribed for a relatively low cost. Consider this as a marketing expense, in reverse. Government agencies publish their requirements as Sources Sought, RFI, and RFP solicitations; these advertisements are usually freely available to the public. The challenge is the number of them; no single government-operated procurement clearing house exists. Instead, there are 1000s of them across the US.

Government-Provided Services and Access

All levels of government provide some electronic access to public solicitations. Some are better than others, and all are substandard compared to the quality of information systems that most private companies are accustomed to, particularly in cloud computing and software.

The most common "gap" among the government-provided systems is an inability to save search criteria, subscribe to and receive reliable messaging alerts notifying vendors of new opportunities, and minimal search capabilities, usually limited to only the listing description entered by the contracting officer. Private systems, in contrast, will provide the features above and search for keywords inside the solicitation's document attachments, not limited to the posted description.

Beta SAM

Recall from earlier chapters I have mentioned the federal government's System for Award Management (SAM) at www.sam.gov. Historically, the SAM platform served as a vendor registration and vendor business records management. Several years ago, the government embarked on an extensive overhaul of its procurement systems. An early phase of the project included the integration of its procurement opportunities postings. These were published previously as fbo.gov (Federal Business Opportunities) and were added as a new (experimental) feature to the sam.gov platform. The experimental "version" was accessible by the public at https://beta.sam.gov ("Beta Sam"). Despite providing approximately the same information as fbo.gov, the Beta Sam interface seemed to work much better. Humorously, the system and the name caught on within the government procurement and contracting communities. Those of us in software chuckled to ourselves about how often people referred to using "Beta Sam" and wondered if they realized that it was a test & development release of the software. Whatever the circumstances were, as of this writing in mid-2022, the features developed within Beta Sam have now been provided as additional features in a recent release of the production Sam.gov system. Sam.gov serves as a one-stop shop for federal contracting business registration, opportunity advertisements, and historical contract research. Albeit still buggy from my observation.

To search for new opportunities in Sam.gov, browse to https://www.sam.gov; you will want to read the popup describing the end of their use of the DUNS numbers and transition to Unique Entity Identifier. Click on "Contract Opportunities," which is annotated with "previously fbo.gov," and search by contract number, keywords, agency name, or other criteria.

There are quite a few drawbacks to relying on this system for business purposes. First, it doesn't work very well. I can search for opportunity numbers that I am actively bidding on, and I will often not find the opportunity. Often, if I search by the agency, I'll find it in the stack of hundreds from that agency, but not by the keyword or the opportunity ID number. The strange search problems seem to be a common occurrence, and I wouldn't recommend using this in a capacity to sustain your business.

I have one use for it, our "paid-for" privately developed system includes hyperlinks to the Sam.gov opportunity posting, and I'll send that web link to industry partners when discussing an opportunity since we all use different subscription-based private platforms.

FPDS

As strange as Beta Sam is, the Federal Procurement Data System (FPDS) stands in contrast as a handy and better-functioning system. FPDS does not provide active solicitations; instead, it shows procurement information for previously awarded contracts. At a minimum, the purchase order metadata or the award documents, the contracting officer's contact information, and total dollar amounts are provided. Many have the provider's offer or proposal documents as attachments.

Searching in FPDS is simple and effective, but keep in mind there is a LOT of data behind it. That said, the EZ Search "search bar" on the home page of www.fpds.gov works like an Internet search engine and is about as efficient for results.

In previous chapters, I discussed researching likely competitors to estimate where their pricing will be on the current opportunity I am working on, and FPDS is one of the reliable sources that I use for that research.

Sam.gov also seems to be adding the functionality, but I haven't had any luck using it. It appears to require specific information to retrieve a record. I prefer to go "fishing" with a large net.

State-Level Procurement Systems

State procurement systems are either purpose-built custom or semi-custom systems or procured from a Software as a Service provider (SaaS). Standard functionality will include vendor pre-registration and submittal of various documents, such as evidence of insurance coverage, a certificate of good standing from your state's corporation organizing authority, an IRS W-9, and any small business certifications. Some will also remit email alerts for new solicitations that match the specified criteria.

For many jurisdictions, agencies require the submittal of a proposal via the state's procurement system, so be sure to register your company well ahead of the "need." In the worst turnaround times I have experienced, it can take up to 10 days to approve new vendor registrations, so don't wait until the due date of the RFP.

Private Systems

Many private systems are on the market for subscription fees at varied price points. Any of these systems I would consider upgrade over the free government platforms, but none should be considered an endorsement. I have only added the following systems, as I have directly used these in the past. For most, the features and capabilities overlap with one another, but all have strengths and weaknesses. I recommend trying each for yourself and for your budget.

Deltek GovWin IQ

Deltek GovWin IQ (GovWin)[1] is probably the most popular solicitation search service for the federal government market. Deltek also markets a state and local module but lacks some capabilities that make the IQ federal product excellent.

Solicitations in GovWin are very searchable, and a unique feature is their projections of likely future procurements derived from previous procurements and the expiration dates of those contracts in FPDS. GovWin appends this with their live research and follow-up with the agencies and will include notes of their conversations. Contacts provided by GovWin for each solicitation are very accurate.

A unique capability of GovWin is the contractor networking features. GovWin aggregates a contractor database (from sam.gov and fpds.gov) with public sector sales volumes, agencies, and NAICS codes. When in need of a prime, sub, or teammate, GovWin subscribers can go much farther than "a guy the neighbor knows" or "a friend of a friend of a golfing buddy." Instead, GovWin subscribers can search for other contractors that meet specific criteria, such as contracts of values between x and y, current or recent work at a particular agency, and within a specific NAICS code. If your target is a specific opportunity at an individual agency, having a teammate already working at the agency or at least familiar with their procurement staff can be a tremendous advantage. I have used GovWin off and on for many years, but it is also one of the more expensive services.

Add-ons are offered for different contracting tiers, with or without program manager contact records, and a complete package can be pretty expensive.

GovSpend

GovSpend[2] is excellent in ways almost in opposition to the strengths and weaknesses of GovWin. First, GovSpend doesn't provide "precanned" solicitation forecasting but has an excellent previous-awards database. The archived database contains details to line items on purchase orders, contracts, awards, cooperative contracts, and blanket purchase orders. Often with the solicitation and response documents attached. Another notable difference, GovSpend includes the federal, state, and local markets within a single subscription model.

Contacts on GovSpend are good, nearly on par with GovWin, but I have observed some minor gaps. GovSpend's ability to export contact records is different (and better) than GovWin's. Subscribers can download a (large) allowance of government contacts monthly for import into their customer relationship management (CRM) system or email marketing. The same export capability is provided for historical contract data and current opportunities.

As a researcher by background, I prefer the GovSpend product and its business model. While it lacks the "forecasting" features of GovWin, I can also download the same contract historical records to a spreadsheet, keep only the fields I want, and import them into my CRM software for my tracking and forecasting purposes, along with the contracts' points of contact for email or telephone marketing. Again, the same information as GovWin, but with a different presentation method, and I am sure people will have their preferences.

The interface is a different design from the others I have used, it can be counterintuitive at first but works wonderfully when the subscriber gets the hang of it.

CJIS Group

I used CJIS Group[3] for about a year, but it has been several years since. It began life, I think, as a tool that specialized in law enforcement procurement but evolved into a state & local service. The product niche is a lot of original research on state budgets and similar reporting and is very information technology focused. If these are your market interests, this is your tool.

BidSync, BidPrime, BidNet, FindRFP, PublicPurchase, DemandStar, and Others

At the other end of the price spectrum is the more basic services. These used to be very inexpensive, but their pricing has increased in recent years. They are still much more affordable than the premium brands mentioned above.

These are essential search services with basic information and solicitation attachments. You won't find contractor networking in these or the ability to see all of the transactions your competitors did last month or last year, like GovWin and GovSpend offer. What you do get is a cost-efficient service to significantly improve your chances of finding "more" opportunities relevant to your capabilities with a much smaller time investment than the "free" (but time-consuming) government-provided services require.

A word of caution with the lower-priced services, with some brands you may often see service descriptions such as [paraphrasing] "member agencies," and most will have some specifics in terms of states and counties or federal coverage. Ask what is included in the package and if there are any coverage gaps or omissions to your subscription. For example, if you subscribe to a regional state's subscription, ask if they can provide you a list of the agencies included or excluded from coverage and if there is a fee to download specific solicitation documents after you locate one of interest. This isn't a negative, rather, just be informed about the market coverage included with what you are buying.

For companies getting started in government contracting with a very straightforward approach to search for, download, and respond to RFPs, the lower-priced services are an excellent place to start.

I suggest trying several before subscribing to one. All have strengths and weaknesses, which come down to how your marketing and sales process will work.

---

1. GovWin IQ. (2022). https://iq.govwin.com/neo/home.
2. GovSpend. (2022). https://govspend.com/.
3. CJIS Group. (2022). https://www.cjisgroup.com/.

PART V

PROPOSAL PLANNING AND WRITING

8

THE FIRST PROPOSAL

Using the method in previous chapters, you should have shredded the requirements in your RFP, RFQ, or RFI and documented each as a requirement to be addressed in your proposal. Following, those requirements should now reside within an outline of your proposal designed to comply with the response content and order specifications, as stated in the solicitation.

Before I begin my first draft, I'll do one more review and edit the outline. Often I will make collaborative changes at the suggestion of others that seemed like a great idea at the time but suddenly looked different or out of place with fresh eyes. Do you feel good about it now? Ok, let's get started.

The software you use for writing is really at your preference, and I will not speak to anything in particular. Instead, I'll stick to generalities common to all word processing software.

Basic Document Setup

Everyone has seen "word art" in documents, and it always looks like "word art," so take it up a notch. If this is your first proposal, the total effort to design a world-class proposal template will probably not be worth it for a single proposal effort. Instead, I recommend you start with an attractive template that looks like you sell stuff for a living and evolve to meet your needs over time.

Before you begin, set up your document. If you have a graphics person assisting you, they (should) have implemented your company's stylesheet as part of the template. For example, you should configure font, color, and size specifications for each type style. I recommend using standard fonts and avoiding trying to be artistic. The reason? If the font is not installed on the reader's computer, it will self-select whatever the default is. When that happens, your layout will instantly change, your page breaks will move, and it may suddenly look terrible. Stick to the basics: Arial, times, or other common ones.

If you do not have a company template to use, here are a couple of options:

Buy Something

If this is your first proposal, the total effort to design a world-class proposal template will probably not be worth the advantage of a single bid. Instead, I recommend you start with something relatively complete and evolve to meet your needs over time.

If you do a web search for whatever software you use and "proposal template," you will probably get a lot of options. I don't recommend "free" ones because there is always a catch, a virus introduced into your computer, an incomplete template, or something else negative. Pay a little and get something that you like that is complete and professionally designed.

Some software will have built-in templates, and these can work as well. Be careful not to use something too obviously over-used by others. For example, we have all seen the 5 or 10 most popular resume layouts, and they all look exactly the same.

Configure It

Next, pull up the Styles applet for your document. How to do so will vary by product, but you should be able to use the online help to find it if you do not already know. You should see a variety of Type Styles - "Normal," "Body Text," "Heading 1," "Heading 2," and others are common.

Start with Heading 1 and click or select to "modify" the style. Heading 1 will be your topmost "heading" for the document organization. Headings are used like steps in your outline; heading 1 will always be the top level, just below a "title." Configure heading 1 with a style you like for your document. When satisfied, save it, and move on to the next. At a minimum, you will need about three or four layers of headings, the "normal" text or "body," captions, title, subtitle, lists, table text, and a bullet text type if included. If you have noticed that some people do "double carriage returns" between paragraphs or use too many very tight single-spacing or odd-looking paragraph widths, this is usually due to improperly configured type styles or not defining them.

You may notice that you can configure the height before and after the style, so, for example, you can increase the space below a heading or between paragraphs. Now do this for the other type styles, and you will have already mastered 50% of the advantage of using a word processor versus an old typewriter.

Some jurisdictions will require hard copies, and some subsets may require specific types of paper to be used. If the RFP or a policy referenced by the RFP requires it, make sure you have those materials on hand.

Pro Tip: Research papers in school were great for learning how to write, but have you ever seen a sales brochure that looks like a term paper? You don't want your proposal to look like one, either.

Pro Tip: Start with a professional proposal template, whether purchased or produced internally. The layout, graphics, colors, and type styles should be designed to sell.

Typical Proposal Contents

All solicitations and proposals are unique, but most of them will have several common sections.

Title Page

I like simple but beautiful title pages. It's your document, so it is your choice, but I'll provide some tips as I see them. Everyone has seen "word art" in documents, and it always looks like "word art," so don't use that on your title page. From experience, you don't want to go over the top with many rich graphics unless you have the time to monitor the output quality. Rich colors and rich photographs can create print & production problems at the tail end if you need to produce hard copies. A busy background can make reading the text in front of it very difficult. Plain will also look too "plain," striking a balance is an art in and of itself.

I include all the basic solicitation and bidder information on the title page. I'll do a graphic on the top half, and predominantly a blend of the company's logo with whatever font and color scheme I am presently using, and the solicitation information in the center of the top, the RFP name, solicitation number, and other relevant details if applicable, such as a blanket purchase agreement number.

The bottom half will have a text box with nested tables containing the company's name, address, NAICS codes, website, phone numbers, DUNS number, CAGE code, and contact information.

Some RFPs will require a specific font and text size. Professionally, if I use a template and appearance scheme for the company, I'll keep the title pages the same and only implement the specified font and text size for the document's content. I tend to evolve the title page over time, and changing text font or size can have unintended adverse side effects when using tables or artistic layouts. No one seems to notice or care, so I'll leave the title page as designed when applicable.

Transmittal

Transmittal pages immediately follow a title page. Here, I address the points of contact for the solicitation, thank them for reviewing our proposal, and include any notes needed, such as the number of volumes included, the number of attachments, or other important notices. If I need to take some liberties, I'll also note those. For example, sometimes, a specific pricing table is required, and your pricing model may be challenging to fit into the agency's provided template. Usually, I will be referencing a question submitted or a previous phone conversation where we agreed on this approach, and I'll just be reminding the contracting officer of the permission granted.

Beginning with the transmittal page or each text block, set your type style accordingly. The salutation style you like, the main body of your letter, your signature block, etc. Continue doing this throughout the document. We will discuss why shortly.

Table of Contents

I like to add a table of contents and do so after the transmittal. Why? Because I like the cover letter to be the first thing they see instead of a bunch of lines and page numbers. It's a preference.

Leave the Table of Contents (TOC) until the end, and let your word processor auto-create it. As long as you properly use the type styles you set up, this will be very easy. Most of the writing software packages will allow you to configure the levels of headings to include in your TOC, so if you like an abbreviated TOC, you should only involve heading 1, or if you want more detail, extend to heading 2 or 3 topics. Usually, these are also hyperlinked to the document page referenced automatically, making a PDF sent to the prospective customer elementary to navigate.

Pro Tip: you can avoid the "awkward" inclusion of the Transmittal page in your TOC, which the reader would have just seen on the page prior, by not using a "heading" type style for the "Transmittal" at the top. Instead, use a normal text style and enlarge or bold the font as you prefer.

Pro Tip: sometimes, I prefer to edit the TOC away from the computer-generated version manually. When I do, I'll let the software auto-create it as the last thing on my task list so the page numbers are correct. Then I'll copy the whole thing, delete it, and paste it back as "text" to edit as I please.

Executive Summary

My next page is usually the Executive Summary. I'll create the heading here when doing my draft, but that is it. Why? Because this summarizes your proposal, and if you haven't written it yet, there is nothing to digest. Create the placeholder here, and the Executive Summary should be your last section written.

A vital ingredient of the executive summary is stating your understanding of the requirement. Explain your understanding of the agency's needs, the problem to be solved, or the solution to be improved. Summarize their concerns, and then speak to how your proposal addresses those concerns and why your approach should be their first choice.

Technical Proposal

I begin the technical proposal with a few paragraphs of the "about us" boilerplate. The company's history, our essential products, and critical market verticals. Some will place this in the executive summary; I have done both in the past. I am reasoning for placing it in the technical proposal due to page limits. Often the executive summary has a limit of one or two pages, and I want to summarize the offer there. Some readers may initially skim the executive summary, so I want to hook their interest to entice reading the rest in detail. Some company background is needed, but it is hard to get extra points when including it, so don't give up limited space in the executive summary.

After "about us," I'll launch directly into the point-scoring section of the proposal. If a specified order of content is required, it begins now. Or, without the specification, I'll repeat my response to each requirement in the order that I outlined the response. Usually, this will be identical to or very similar to the order each was presented in the solicitation.

For more extended sets of requirements, such as a litany of product feature specifications, which can be summarized with a yes or no response, I'll include a table at the beginning of this section with the caption "evaluators' guide," I'll list out the requirements in separate rows, and place a yes or no response the second column for each. I will then hyperlink each requirement to the page where it is addressed.

How the requirements are answered will depend entirely upon your company, your industry, and what you are selling. In my opinion, there is no right or wrong, only the quality of the message, delivery, and your strategy to maximize the points granted for each answer.

Project Plan

Project plans, integration plans, and implementation plans are the same thing with different names. The project plan will convince the customer that you have carefully planned the integration of your solution, the conversion of their existing provider's services to yours, or the delivery of the products on time.

Many government procurements will specify a particular management approach or a quality of service delivery. Whether it is a project management methodology, a service ticket request, a delivery process, or an industry standard to follow, it is a best practice to integrate those requirements into your project plan without doing so at such a technical level to intimidate a reader.

Roles and Responsibilities

Some projects can be complex interactions between the contractor and government staff. Weapon systems, software development, or intelligence gathering systems would undoubtedly be some examples out of many possible. When this interaction is necessary and expected, it is an excellent practice to itemize "who does what" so the evaluators can easily understand your offer. The description can be a table, workflow chart, or narrative. Be clear and concise, and eliminate any areas of uncertainty.

Quality Assurance (QA)

Problems will arise for a long-term staffing engagement, software development project, or commodity delivery contract. Your plan to detect defects before they manifest, correct a delayed shipment, or fix a software bug is just as important as the delivery of the product or service itself. If the solicitation doesn't ask, including your QA plan is a good practice. If it does ask, you must include your QA plan.

Suggestions for QA may include empowering your project team to make decisions at the lowest possible level for efficiency of operation, sampling every tenth product off the assembly line, or whatever is the standard for your industry.

Training Plan

If your product or service requires training to use, operate, or access, include your approach to providing that training. Standard practices are on-site and in-person, including training materials.

Customizations

Earlier in my career, customizations seemed to be expected to match the agency's specific workflow or expectations. Indeed, this is expensive to do in terms of "people time," and outcomes are not always "better." If your solution requires customizations to meet the requirements, document your approach, available resources, and delivery expectations.

Security Plan

Many government projects require levels of data or information security to be maintained. No one wants to be the subject of tomorrow's newspaper headlines, so an expectation to keep your customer's confidence goes without saying.

In your security plan, stipulate the requirements from the RFP and how you meet them. Commonly these requirements are answered with various security certifications you maintain, compliance with requirements specified in the agency's security manual, or conditions stated in the solicitation.

Address these requirements completely.

Value-Added Capabilities

Your technical proposal has addressed the product or service requirements, customizations, project plan, training, QA, and ensuring the customer's security. What else do you do that your competitors do not and were not mentioned in the solicitation? If the product already includes it, it never hurts to say it.

Some jurisdictions have strict guidelines against spending more on unneeded capabilities. So including these can be a double-edged sword. If you include this section, convey the features are already present and included in the product with no added cost.

Pro Tip: requirements are often described as "mandatory" and "preferred." If your capabilities are missing any mandatory requirements, carefully review the solicitation or ask whether the agency can move those specific requirements to "preferred." If the solicitation specifies a disqualification for missing any of these mandatory items, or the contracting officer is unwilling to waive them, consider adding a subcontractor to assist you or reconsider submitting the offer and looking for an opportunity better suited to your skills.

Pro Tip: I don't think I have ever received feedback on my approach to indexing my proposals with an evaluators' guide or a table of contents, but they seem much easier to read. Often the evaluation panel will split up the review sections, and taking this approach enables an easy sharing of the work without the risk of "missing" something and subsequently the loss of points for the requirement.

Pro Tip: some companies and evaluators prefer to read where a type of service has been done for other customers, such as an inline citation to a specific reference. "We will do XYZ and have previously demonstrated our capacity for doing so at [reference cited #1]." Most solicitations require a small handful of references. Continuously citing them throughout the document makes for a difficult read and even more challenging to evaluate. If it is necessary for your industry, add a column to your evaluators' guide table and cite each reference where you have performed the work before.

Pro Tip: write out each requirement in whole or paraphrased format. You will probably score better if the reader doesn't have to flip back and forth between the RFP and your answer.

Key Staff

Whether you sell products or services, you commonly see a requirement to provide information regarding your "key staff." In some cases, the "key staff" individuals will be explicitly identified by title, role, or requirements; other times, the identification of the "key staff" will be at the discretion of the proposer.

Some types of contracts are more amenable to doing this than others. For example, construction companies can pick up their subcontractors and full-time employees and move from one project to the next after completion. Technology companies that perform long-term multi-year on-site services engagements have considerably less flexibility.

When the "key staff" are specified, the proposer is expected to provide resumes of people on staff that will be assigned in the defined roles if selected for the contract. In practice, particularly for a large contract, contractors don't have dozens or hundreds of people sitting on the bench waiting for billable work - you may need to do some soft recruiting of new potential hires or look at people in your organization that you can re-assign. In the worst case, you can show "sample resumes" of people you would not assign to the contract or, even worse, your proposed job descriptions. The agency will evaluate your proposal heavily on this. The gold star is people ready, willing, and able in the local area - and your scoring will go down from there. "Key staff" resumes are about establishing your credibility to perform.

For opportunities allowing the proposer to specify their key staff, the best practice is to identify your existing program or project manager to be assigned, with a complete resume and your executive leadership within the chain of command above the project manager. You may also want to provide people with critical skills that the candidate will need - your lead software developer, a data scientist, your senior architect, or whatever is appropriate for the opportunity.

Above all, pay close attention to the education and experience requirements if they are stated. Most government agencies are particular about educational minimums. While you may consider a certain number of years of experience instead of a bachelor's or master's degree, if this is not stated as allowed, do not take that liberty. If your preferred person does not meet the minimum standards, use another person for the proposal, or you will risk disqualification. After the award, do not unilaterally make the switch to your preferred. Request the modification through the contracting officer.

Cost Proposal

The agency may request cost proposals to be submitted within a single technical volume or presented as a separate volume. Be sure to note the requirement in the RFP.

Often solicitations will indicate that cost is not a concern, not a significant concern, or some flavor of stating that. In my experience, it is always an important concern. The reason is how the evaluation scorecards work.

Unqualified offers will be eliminated during initial screening or early in the evaluation process. Almost universally, The contracting officer will grant the most points (for cost) to the lowest priced offer from among the qualified offers. For example, the lowest bid may get 30 points, the next-lowest 25, and the second-lowest 20. All offers receive points for the price submitted, but if the total scorecard is 100 points, and your offer gives up 10 points to the lowest bidder, it could be tough to come back from that and prevail.

The content and approach of your cost proposals will vary. Professional services offers are straightforward, emphasizing labor types, hourly rates, and annual hours. Commodity and supplies offers should include shipping and delivery costs or details specified in the solicitation. Software or other publications should consist of or reference an exhibit for the subscription agreement.

Often a cost proposal template is provided, and I will typically include that in a document with a narrative as an insert and separately have a copy of the cost quote file if it is an editable spreadsheet file.

Pro Tip: When quoting professional services for government contracts, be realistic about how many hours your people are on the job annually. Simple math suggests 2,080 hours per year (52 x 40 hours per week), but your people will not be working on government holidays, sick days, or during their vacation leave. To be competitive with other offers, quote the hours accordingly.

References

Be aware your past performance is a large portion of the evaluation of the bid or proposal. At a minimum, references are a pass or fail consideration and are almost always evaluated with a substantial percentage of the points tallied within the evaluation scorecard. The scoring of references in the public sector differs from the commercial industry. Commercial customers are often referred to your business, seek you out independently, respond to your marketing, or review comments about your business on social media. The government requires "proof" that you can fully perform on your offer and do so with high quality. Note that a typical value of your provided references will be around 30% of the possible total evaluation points on the scorecard. If you do poorly here, it is unlikely you can put together an offer sufficiently compelling to overcome the deficit. Commercial buyers will usually review proposals from one to three providers, the government will likely see a dozen or more offers to choose from, and you can't afford to lose a single point and remain in the running.

The gold standard for past performance scoring will be providing the number of references requested with the same product or service scope of work, provided for another similar government agency, completing the contract on time and budget, with a referenced contract number, and the agency that purchased, the value, and the contracting officer's contact information for verification and clarification of your claims. The contracting officer will contact your references. If he or she cannot reach one or more contacts, you risk the reference being voided, so speak to your references ahead of time. Ask them if you may provide their contact information to another prospective customer for this purpose. I do not recommend doing so without their permission. If you only have a few references and they are unwilling to cooperate, this will be a hurdle you will need to develop a strategy for before moving on.

Below other government contracts as references, commercial references can be submitted but are customarily considered the lowest value for evaluation purposes because an external review cannot fully evaluate them. For example, if three references are required, most contracting officers will score commercial references as a lower quality of reference than a fully verifiable government reference.

Government buyers prefer to see that you have previously managed the complexity of competition for performing, tracking, invoicing, and closing a government contract satisfactorily. More than all other considerations, government agencies are very risk-averse, and few are willing to "go first" with a new vendor.

At a minimum, you need several excellent commercial customer references to be viable. If you don't have them, GSA Schedule 70 offers a "Springboard" consideration for new companies to qualify for the FSS, though competing for an opportunity will require past performance.

In the worst case, if you do not have at least three high-quality commercial references, the contracting officer can use the owner's resume to reference previous work under some circumstances and for some agencies. However, the company's owner will have to be the "key staff" assigned to the contract for day-to-day operations. This requirement cannot be substituted and is typically for an owner-operator startup with no other previous business activity.

For larger established businesses where operation of the contract by your staff is expected, commercial references are required.

If you cannot provide references, you have some other options, but you will need a teammate to succeed.

RFP Response Responsiveness

There are two parts to the evaluation of the offers. Responsiveness is usually a pass-fail question. Did the offeror respond with the required information, specifications, supporting documents, and pricing? If you miss any, you are at risk of being declared non-responsive and disqualified during the first phase of the evaluation. In practice, I innocently omitted a disclosure type of the document, which was only a clerical error. The contracting officer also assumed so and just emailed me a request for it, which I immediately sent. Some of these requirements can have 30 or 40 documents to complete. Mistakes happen, the government's document upload service can be buggy, file attachments can get mangled, and stuff happens. Almost every contracting officer I have ever known is a reasonable person, and some will quietly agree that the process can be over-encumbering and accommodating to all responding contractors at the front end of the initial submittal deadline. I always email a list of what they should have received and ask for a statement of receipt and verification. If something is missing, it is easily fixed before they begin their evaluation.

The second part of the evaluation is the formal scoring of the responses by an evaluation panel. The scoring is usually done objectively, using common measurements for each received proposal. In my experience, the panel members will read each response individually, scoring each with a standardized scorecard. The group will merge their findings and agree on the order of preference for the technical attributes. Some panels may review all of the responses as a group collaboratively.

The third phase, handled quite differently by different agencies, is the cost (or price) proposal review. Some agencies will ask for the pricing to be included as a single proposal document with the technical volume; others will require it to be submitted as a separate volume. Some agencies have multiple or all evaluation panel members review the pricing, others will limit the price scoring to only the contracting officer, and others may limit it to the contracting officer and the executive sponsor whose budget is funding the project.

Planning Your Response

There are three goals for the design of your proposal:

1. Your offer survives the first responsiveness pass/fail phase
2. Maximize the scorecard points during the technical evaluation
3. Maximize the points given for the cost evaluation

Most RFPs will include a description of the proposal evaluation process and scoring methodology, and many will have specific criteria and relative importance. Some requirements may be a pass or fail, a percentage of the total points, or you may see each line item and the maximum points available. Some RFPs will include a sample of the calculation card used by each evaluator, with each scoring factor and an explanation of how it will be calculated. Do you remember a high school or college teacher who "taught you the test?" You get the idea, do that here. Take that sample scorecard or sample scoring and design your proposal to max out the points. You won't see any points offered for creative writing, so stick to the basics.

Shredding the RFP

First, "shred" the RFP. I don't mean to send it into the trash. Instead, dissect it from the beginning to the end. You are looking for all of the statements that state "Contractor Shall," "Contractor Will," "Product Will," "Product Shall," or "Services Will." Every requirement stated must be answered, preferably in the affirmative, within your response or your proposal's statement of work (SOW). Most proposal teams will accumulate these statements, with their paragraph number or page number location, into a spreadsheet or other tracking tool.

I'll include the following when I am "shredding" the RFP. The verbatim (copied and pasted) requirement or statement, the location where I found it in the RFP - usually a paragraph number, a blank column to be completed later indicating where the answer is written in the proposal, who is assigned to writing the response to the requirement, a time estimate to do so or a deadline, and the last column for the cost estimate [for each requirement].

I will include a column for version tracking or a "status" of each requirement for more extraordinary proposal efforts. I prefer to use version numbers. A decimal smaller than 1.0 indicates an "unfinished" response requirement, 0.00 for non-started, 0.25 for the first draft, 0.50 for the second, and 0.75 for awaiting final review. With this approach, I can calculate the average version numbers for the entire column to estimate how far along I am with the proposal document.

You should begin the "shredding" process immediately after publishing the RFP. In addition to the proposal due date, there may be deadlines for questions about the RFP, bidders' meetings, and other calendar deadlines. The scheduling deadline column in your requirements spreadsheet can be used for this or an extra one.

Pro Tip: I like to read the RFP from start to finish and leave my questions and comments in the margins before transferring the requirements to my outline.

Proposal Outline

After documenting the requirements for the solicitation, I will draft a detailed proposal outline. I find it is easier to stay focused on my writing and maintain the organization of the proposal when following an outline of the document. I will spend so much time on my requirements spreadsheet and proposal outline that a week into the proposal writing timeline, others will want to "see the current draft." Truthfully, with my writing style, the proposal outline can be as much as 50% of my first draft effort or more, and I may not have a single word into the proposal template yet, but from a progress perspective, I am pretty far along. Everyone will develop their style and process, but this is what I have found to be the most effective. I also tend to multi-task throughout my day, which is typical for most people. An outline will keep you on target when you find yourself stopping and starting, jumping from one solicitation to another during the same day, attending unrelated meetings, picking up the kids, or catching a flight to a trade show.

Assuming you review the RFP from start to end, your requirements spreadsheet and the proposal outline will look like they will parrot back the RFP requirements in the same order they were written in the RFP, which is fine. Maintaining the same order and organization will make the agency's evaluation easier.

My proposal outline will strongly resemble the requirements spreadsheet but is more of an "annotated version." I'll transfer the RFP requirements into the proposal outline one at a time, expanding each with initial thoughts I have about a response, capturing a few bullet points below each item. These bullet points are initial ideas that suggest the direction I'll use in the first draft of the proposal. There is value in looking at the requirements and revisiting your initial approach to each a day or two later. Your frame of thought may be different, other requirements from the RFP may frame your proposal theme differently, or you can be subliminally distracted one time but not the other. These external influences are never apparent at the time but are evident later.

I have two reasons for using an outlining software tool for drafting my outlines instead of a word processor. First, I find the outlining apps to be "simple software" without many bells and whistles, and I won't waste time on distractions like which bullet style, font, or numbering conventions look better. Second, the outlining apps allow you to drag and drop items and their subitems to reposition them wherever you want. Although this is a personal preference, I find it more efficient than bulky software designed for spelling and grammar checks. An unrelated minor benefit, outline apps usually have a mobile device companion version, and if I have a random new idea later when away from my computer, I can always add it somewhere in the proposal outline.

Outlining Curveballs

Some RFPs specify a proposal content order. Usually, this will be provided in the "how to respond" or "submission instructions" section. You saw that and added it as a general requirement when doing your RFP shred, right? I usually don't like these because the "order" is frequently awkward or does not flow well from the contractor's perspective. Consequently, I find these to be harder to plan, and the proposal will not read as well as if I wrote it freehand. I don't think of that opinion as arrogant; agency contracting staff write RFPs, and I write dozens of proposals yearly. We each have our areas of expertise.

If the proposal has a specified content order and format, I will usually ignore the RFP's response specification while crafting my requirements spreadsheet and creating my first draft of the proposal outline. Trying to jump around the RFP paragraphs to pull the requirements out in an order that matches the specified proposal content order is a recipe for a lot of additional [wasted] time and the risk of missing something.

Instead, I'll draft my requirements spreadsheet by reading through the RFP as I usually would, itemizing each requirement, noting its RFP location, making content assignments and deadlines, and completing the other columns for the requirements spreadsheet.

Next, I'll draft my proposal outline as I usually would, transferring the requirements into sections and headings within the proposal outline and adding my commentary and initial thoughts.

Finally, this is where the outlining app shines. The outlining app will take everything below each heading that I move and paste it to the new location as a single object. I'll copy my first completed outline to a "version 2" file and then drag & drop the outline sections to match the order of the RFP's outline or content order specifications.

Using this approach, I will already have all of the requirements in my tracking spreadsheet, I will already have those requirements trans-ferred into the proposal outline as I usually would, and now I am just dragging the pieces & parts en masse to where they need to go. Voila, no stress, no mess.

Pricing

I begin my pricing calculations following the proposal outline and before the first draft of the proposal itself. There are two reasons for doing so. First, I use the outline as input to build my rough pricing and cost analysis. This is particularly important for professional services or labor contracts; each row of the outline will generally be a work requirement and can later be converted into units of time (labor hours) and, subsequently, a price. Second, in some cases, I will price and submit the proposal myself without input from others; in other cases, I'll need information and opinions from subject matter experts for products or services within their area of expertise.

Cost versus Price

The government will use "cost proposal" and "price proposal" interchangeably, but for the sake of this writing, I will not.

Cost is what your product or service "costs" your company to build or deliver. The public sector market is very competitive, and you need to understand your costs.

Price is what you expect to charge for your product or service. Sometimes cost is a direct input to fees, such as professional services and labor contracts, construction contracts, or cost-plus agreements. For others, price is a calculation of supply versus demand. In other words, "What will the customer pay?"

Establishing Cost

The draft proposal outline is my primary tool for establishing a rough proposal price. I'll add two columns, Cost per Unit (of work or product) and Quantity.

Scrolling down the outline and reviewing each task item individually is an efficient way to establish an overall cost of performing the contract. Calculate using the unit cost and quantity, whether labor hours or your product's internal cost.

Suppose input from other team members is needed to establish the cost of any items. In that case, it is precious to start the cost and price calculation as soon as the outline is completed, and any collaborative or research efforts needed for establishing your pricing plan may continue in parallel with the proposal writing phase.

Competitive Pricing Research

Researching competitors in the public sector is straightforward using some of the tools we discussed in the previous chapter. Ideally, the agency has held a bidders' conference, and now we can use the photo of the attendees' sign-in sheet to do some quick research on each.

Look for recent contracts and marketing materials for each attendee, and if you have typical competitors in your market, look at their contracts and materials too.

I prefer to record the information of interest from competitors' contracts and catalogs in a spreadsheet, making the best attempt to line up "similar" across the rows, so I can develop an average price tag that competitors are getting. Be sure to pay close attention to contract dates, and annual escalations may increase the cost from the original base year price; look for those.

Price Proposal

The price proposal will be unique for your industry and solicitation, but determining the competitors' likely price range, your costs, and the minimum margin you will accept if awarded is similar across all sectors.

I will determine two more numbers, the minimum profit margin by adding another column to the proposal outline; and the average competitors' price for like products or services from any recent contract pricing research.

Tips for Labor Pricing

It can take a newcomer to the public sector several failed attempts before becoming competitive in public sector services contracts. I can provide a few trade tricks to save effort and provide better profitability simultaneously.

First, calculate when your people will actually be providing the services. For most, this will not include holidays, paid vacation days, an average number of sick days every year, or weekends. There are differences, such as road repair or snow removal, but for most government services, a rule of thumb is 1920 hours per year. If you calculate 52 weeks per year and 40 hours per week, you will use 2,080 hours, and your quote will be much higher than your competitors.

Second, be sure to incorporate your loaded labor cost into your pricing. Government contracting services are almost required full-time, so your employees' vacations, holidays, sick leave, medical appointments, and family leave days, if not allowed in the billing, will have to be incorporated into your hourly labor rates.

Third, if travel is required, understand how it will be paid for. The solicitation will sometimes specify separate reimbursable invoicing will be processed for travel-related expenses (and related limits), or you may be required to factor it into your labor pricing.

And last, everything takes longer than you think in government. Long-term software development projects will be filled with [many] planning and status meetings every week; materials inspections for road construction projects may not happen exactly when you need them to, and projects that require a lot of travel will inevitably run into many travel-related delays. I avoid the minutia by calculating each staff member in days, weeks, months, or years.

Pro Tip: I look for competitors' contracts in public records. Any time I see a competitor's recent state contract award, a schedule award, or anything similar, I grab and store them. Finding them in a hurry when I need them never seems to go as well as planned.

Pro Tip: I like to use a shared spreadsheet using a collaborative platform and share my research with others on the team.

Proposal Writing

Before beginning your proposal draft, you shouldn't wait until the end of the Question & Answer (Q&A) cycle. Usually, time is of the essence, and there should be plenty of requirements you can work on that do not require clarification.

You will adopt a draft writing process that works for you. I'll describe mine here.

The First Draft

My first draft begins by inserting my main idea below each heading in the outline where I don't already have one. My first draft responses for each requirement are a sentence or two with the main idea for the answer I intend to provide. If I need others in the organization to expand on these answers from their specific areas of expertise, I'll send each a digest of their required inputs. In my experience, this approach has worked as well as any other. In every company I have worked for, assistance from others outside the public sector sales and marketing group has always been marginally reliable. It's rare to find a technical person that writes well and rarer to find one that puts the sales effort near the top of the priority list. Keep the requests simple, minimize the back & forth, follow up with another email or a phone call if you need, and give them a deadline to respond. I use "soft targets" for deadlines whenever possible, giving myself an extra week after the target I provide. Leave yourself some room in the deadline to rewrite what you get.

Most federal contractors will refer to the first draft as the "Blue Team." The blue team is a starting point. The goal is to get something down on paper, converting your outline into the beginning of each section. I aim to implement the document template and style sheet, create all headings, bullets, and heading numbers, and add notes or comments for others to follow (if it is a team effort). I also like to insert the RFP's relevant requirement for each question or section as a comment in the margin or as an inline annotation that I'll remove later. I do this for a convenient reference, avoiding the need to flip back and forth to the RFP document.

Some sections and answers may be better than others; some will be a skeleton or a placeholder while I wait for supporting input from others. That is fine. The minimum should be your "approach" to each requirement with placeholders for what you need to get from other people. If there has been a previous discussion about the requirement, I'll paste in relevant notes that I have taken with some yellow highlighting or another obvious annotation formatting.

When the blue team draft is completed, circulate it for comment. I also include technical support resource mentions, as they act as a psychological "we are moving on this, and here's the spot your answer will go." I will annotate these spots with labels such as "To be Provided by so & so" (in bold). I usually spend about 1-2 days on a blue team version, regardless of the length of the eventual document.

Second Draft

Federal contractors will call the second draft the "red team." The red team version is complete when all sections have a second-draft answer. Red team drafts are also referred to as "content complete" and will include your technical supplements from others. Other supporting documents, such as insurance certificates, service level agreements, sample terms & conditions, bonding, etc., should also be ready and available. TIP: You may want to avoid inserting supporting documents, charts, or graphs into your proposal until the final draft version for the usability of the document file. In my experience, even with very powerful laptops and desktops, many large document and graphic insertions will drag down the usability and reliability of the word processing file. The rise of cloud document storage, document sharing, collaboration, and working from home (with somewhat limited upload bandwidth) has only exacerbated the problem. Instead, have graphics and external documents identified and in a server folder at this stage and drop in highlighted annotated comments for where each will be placed as a reminder. This approach also allows revisions on those documents if needed, without the added effort of correcting the master document. You can add hyperlinks as placeholders to pull up the documents from a subfolder for convenient collaborative review.

When the red team draft is complete, all proposal stakeholders should read and review all sections and insert their comments, changes, or corrections. Ideally, I am completing the red team version of the proposal approximately when the Q&A questions and answers are posted. Changes to responses suggested by new information found in the Q&A or a newly issued RFP addendum will be added to my next version. I highly recommend using a document sharing and collaboration tool rather than emailing the proposal document back and forth to everyone. "Email-driven" collaboration is slow, will inevitably lead to versioning problems, and someone's changes and comments seem to get skipped or received too late to integrate. Microsoft SharePoint[1] and Google Docs[2] are the most common choices. There are professional proposal writing software suites on the market, and I have tried several of them. Unless you have a lot of proposal volume with large and complex documents, the cost and overhead of working with specialized proposal software systems will probably be more effort than the time saved drafting the documents. Almost everyone I know or have worked with uses Microsoft or Google software. The advantage of these systems is multiple people can be working on documents in real-time, and the changes are updated (relatively) smoothly to everyone else in the background. The software is widespread, and everyone knows how to use it and contribute.

Third Draft

In the third proposal version, commonly referred to as the "gold team," the comments, annotations, suggestions, changes, spelling, and grammatical errors identified in the red team review phase are addressed, removed, or completed. There should be zero remaining extraneous comments or placeholders for external material. All document formatting is finalized, illustrations are added, tables are constructed, supporting documents are attached, and the gold team version begins to resemble what will be submitted to the customer. The only thing I usually skip is the final typesetting, pagination, and header placements. Any final addition or deletion of content will affect the pagination, so it is always my last step.

The gold team review is complex and can be time-consuming. I will reduce the stakeholders here to only the people who are most experienced in the sales process and have been thoroughly involved throughout the proposal draft. Usually, the looming due date doesn't allow time to re-hash technical content or approaches, as that boat has already sailed. That is what the "red team" version is. It's also hard to review your work after staring at the same document for several days or weeks, so I highly recommend that an excellent technical writer or editor reviews the gold team if you have one in your organization. Failing that, I recommend the paid version of Grammarly (not the free one). I use Grammarly daily in my work, but I do not blindly accept every recommendation it makes. I use it to identify spots to look at, and I may take its suggestion or rephrase it with a third alternative. Can I edit my work? Sure, but I also know I'll miss a lot as I usually multitask and read at a pretty fast clip, so I'll skip over details.

Final Draft

A day or two before the due date or shipping date, if a hard copy is required, I refer to it as a "white glove." Any final changes are completed, headers are perfect, footers and legalese is read through, page numbering is added, pagination for readability, tables of contents, bibliographies, indexing, and margins are set for the type of print and publish (if required). When the document is ready, I'll print a hard copy on my laser printer and do the last page-flip walkthrough. I'm only looking for the pagination and headings; surprisingly, documents often print slightly differently from how it looks on the screen; and the final version may need minor tweaks. I recommend only submitting portable document format (PDF) versions of your proposal, which will eliminate formatting, font, and pagination problems related to different software versions or operating systems.

Once satisfied, I will always outsource the final hard copy production to a local printing company. I know many people do it themselves or may have support within their company to do so, and I respect those viewpoints. Trying to print and bind the thing is an extra level of "frazzle" that I don't need and is very cheap to let the experts do. They have excellent paper instead of whatever cheap stuff is loaded in your printer, no one is sending some random print job in the middle of your complex printing and packaging, no toner shortages or weird streaking from the low-quality laser printer, and they always have all of the binding materials on hand. Believe it or not, many agencies will specify the type of paper to submit your response; some require recycled post-consumer waste to be used, others require 32 lb laser, or the RFP may specify four or eight or even ten copies to be submitted. All bound, ten copies of a 50-page proposal is a long day of work and many paper cuts. Usually, by this point, I need to work on the following solicitation, not spend two days printing and shipping the last one. The pros can do the same thing in an hour, and if it doesn't look right, I have them fix it.

Many agencies request an emailed proposal or upload the document to the procurement website. These are ideal, as you have until the deadline to complete your response.

Last Notes

A few last notes about your proposal. First, if you are submitting hard copies, your "deadline" is about three business days before the due date. You must have the hard copy produced, packaged, shipped, and received by the contracting officer before the due date. If shipping something from the West coast to the East coast, "overnight" shipping often isn't "overnight." For me to reach the East coast, for example, my local shipping cutoff is 5 pm, which is costly to send. It is about ½ or ¼ of the price to send the same package as a two-day, but if you must, you must. When I have one of the sales team geographically located closer to the customer, I'll send the print job to a printer in their area instead of my own. Then I'll ask the local salesperson to pick it up, review it, and ship it from the in-region location rather than risk the delivery of a transcontinental package shipment or the cost.

For emailed or uploaded submissions, be wary of your document file size. Email systems will usually reject attachments over 10 or 20 megabytes, and often, the websites don't like large files. You may need to split your submission into several files or use a tool to compress the file. Build some time into the end of your schedule to make these adjustments.

---

1. Microsoft SharePoint (Microsoft Office 365) [Computer Software]. https://www.microsoft.com/en-us/microsoft-365/sharepoint/collaboration.
2. Google Docs (Google Workspace) [Computer Software]. https://www.google.com/docs/about/.

PART VI

WHEN THINGS GO RIGHT

9

PERFORMING YOUR CONTRACT

The importance of performing your contract well and by the letter of the scope of work cannot be understated.

Federal contract performances are reported to the Contractor Performance and Rating System (CPARS) and are visible to all other Federal contracting officers. If you have ever used a social media tool to look at some local restaurants in the area and you find yourself skipping over the ones with horrible reviews - you know how a poor CPARS rating will affect your future competitiveness. Past performance references are also required for every proposal, and Federal contracting officers will look at your CPARS report, in addition to the proposal references provided. If you cherry-pick glowing references to include in the past performance section of your RFP response, but the preponderance of your past and recent work is poorly rated on CPARS, you will invariably be evaluated very poorly on your offers' scorecards. The poor past performance quickly equals less or zero future public sector revenue.

Resolving Challenges

Problems can always happen. Mistakes are made; employees are "people" and make mistakes, or worse, they can become mentally unstable and take it out on your customer. Whatever happens, own it, fix it (immediately), and move on. Make sure their last memory of your performance is not the terrible hire you made that didn't show up 4 out of 5 days a week.

Project Staffing

Employees and staffing on government contracts are critical. Contract pricing needs to be sufficient to afford to hire qualified people who represent your company well, yet not so expensive as to devour your profit. If you are working on a contract for national defense and the project requires security clearances, I wouldn't recommend having a staff of non-resident immigrants show up on day one. They may be legally able to work in the US, but if they have a non-US passport in their wallet, the likelihood of obtaining a US security clearance will be nil. Likewise, convicted felons, recent drunk-driving arrests, personal financial recklessness, drug abuse, and yes - marijuana usage, even if legal locally, are all things that will "not fly" with federal government contracts and the required security clearances.

Make it easier on your company and guarantee your high performance on the contract by researching these types of issues, surveying the labor market as part of your proposal pricing process, and planning to hire appropriately. Several websites specialize in areas of concern to the federal government for security clearances of various levels; the information is not hard to find.

Problem Employees Assigned to Government Contracts

It can be tricky to resolve if you have a problem employee. The employee has labor rights, and you will have to work around those. It would help if you also got them off the government's premises and quickly replaced them with someone that meets the contract's standards. Depending on the employment rules in your state, this may mean that you need to bench the problem for a few weeks while disciplining them or terminate and replace them. Your human resources will need to be involved; I am far from an expert in this area.

You are a service provider, and the government is buying a service; it is your employee, not theirs. Nonetheless, you must perform on your contract, which is job one. If the contracting officer or their representative notifies you that so-and-so needs to be removed from the contract, you have little choice. Staff quality is part of the risk you take.

Reducing Performance Risk

My primary approach to mitigating contract performance risk is always assigning a program manager, our account executive, to "own" the project or engagement. Program managers know their contract inside and out, are responsible for the performance of the scope of work, resolve problems and challenges with the customer as they arise, and manage the day-to-day operation and service delivery. Program managers are most appropriate when on-site professional services are being performed or the value of the goods and services is such that providing a single point of contact that is at least equivalent to the government's contracting officer's qualifications is warranted.

Contracts for products and services provided by your "team" in a primarily off-site capacity can also be enhanced by a program manager role but can also be well-performed by an account manager or account executive role instead. Defining the difference between these titles, I regard them as with versus without a college degree; and whether the person has prior experience working with the government as an internal staff member or contractor. Do you want the person to perform on autopilot for you, or is your periodic or regular involvement welcome in exchange for a lower salary cost?

The point of the person, whichever career level or role you select, is the specialization of the professional to the performance of the contract and "one throat to choke" for the government's contracting officer. For example, if you have a problem with your hotel room when traveling, you don't want to be bounced around from one person to the next looking for an answer on some 1-800 customer service number; you want to talk to the person at the reception desk and get it handled or replaced, not told to go and use a phone lobby phone and speak to someone in a call center somewhere. My point here is the same, the government's contracting officer will want to talk to your company's representative assigned to them.

Singing for Your Supper, the Contract "Recompete"

The "recompete" is when you get to sing for your supper again. Hopefully, only because your base contract and all of the extensions are expiring. If your extensions have not been fully exercised and the opportunity is going out to bid again, this can be a bad sign. I have only had a single instance in my career where this has occurred, and it wasn't due to anything wrong. Our reseller/teammate company was being dissolved because an incoming administration had appointed their CEO to a senior US government administration position, and dissolving the government contracting engagements was a condition of doing so. In that single instance, we successfully won the recompile and continued with the contract, absent our former teammate.

Assuming "bad" has not happened, and the government has just exercised its last extension on your contract, this becomes a great time to talk to your contracting officer. Suppose you have been executing well and your program manager has regularly met with the contracting officer or contracting officer's representative. In that case, your program manager will already know your competitive status, what the government agency would like changed in the following procurement, and your strategy to win again and retain the business. The open line of communication ensured by a qualified program manager cannot be understated here at this phase of the contract's lifecycle.

Hypothetical Example

Suppose you have a five-year contract configured as one base year with four "option" years. For the last four years, your contracting officer has reliably sent you a task order, award letter, purchase order, or some other instrument to extend your contract for another year. You are now early in the fourth option year, and the contracting officer asks for your input on the technical and staffing requirements to perform the contract. Documenting the services you provide is an excellent sign. I also recommend providing some specifications for capabilities unique to your company that may reduce the potential competition if used in the next contract procurement's scope of work or requirements specifications. For now, suffice to say that you should describe the work your company is providing, an approximation of the people involved and their approximate education levels and skillsets, and the number of hours you perform annually or other critical performance indicators relevant to your pricing strategy.

Over time, the cost of technology certainly comes down, the cost of commodities may rise or fall, and many other economic changes occur over five years or more. By law, ongoing requirements performed by a contractor must be periodically re-bid to ensure the taxpayers are getting the best value or price. The recompete also allows you to "catch up" with your pricing compared to your staff's ever-increasing wage, salary, and benefits costs.

In my experience, this is not the time to get greedy either. You are performing your contract well, you know the work, your staff is in place, you have a good relationship with the customer, and it's usually best to set the goal of keeping the revenue in place. Your proposal should essentially write itself. Pull out the original version that won the business five years ago, update it with the assistance of your program manager as a critical contributor (and now you see the importance of that role), and price it to fit your revenue targets for the contract while balancing the budgetary expectations of the customer, also likely to be known by the program manager.

The best way to increase a contract's profit is through improved efficiency, not exorbitant price increases. Use the average staff turnover to move some people around with the top skills in the most-needed positions while using lower-skill levels where the talent isn't needed, and you can make better margins. With several years, the work should be pretty automatic.

PART VII

WRAPPING UP

CONGRATULATIONS!

You have reached the end of this introductory book, be sure to watch for expanded topics that will soon follow.

BIBLIOGRAPHY

Acquisition.gov. (2022). https://www.acquisition.gov/far/19.705-7.

BidNet. (2022). https://www.bidnet.com/.

BidPrime. (2022). https://www.bidprime.com/.

BidSync (Periscope S2G). (2022). https://www.periscopeholdings.com/s2g.

CJIS Group. (2022). https://www.cjisgroup.com/.

DemandStar. (2022). https://network.demandstar.com/.

Ferman, M. (2022, October 8). Texas bans local, state government entities from doing business with firms that "boycott" fossil fuels. The Texas Tribune, https://www.texastribune.org/2022/08/24/texas-boycott-companies-fossil-fuels/.

FindRFP. (2022). https://findrfp.com/.

Google Docs (Google Workspace) [Computer Software]. https://www.-google.com/docs/about/.

GovSpend. (2022). https://govspend.com/.

GovWin IQ. (2022). https://iq.govwin.com/neo/home.

Grammarly (Grammarly Premium) [Computer Software]. https://www.-grammarly.com/premium.

IBISWorld. (2022). https://www.ibisworld.com/us/bed/number-of-busi-nesses/2898/.

Kalanjian, L. (2022). University of Pennsylvania Law School. https://schol-arship.law.upenn.edu/cgi/viewcontent.cgi?article=1710&context=jcl.

Kennedy, M. (2016, March 29). N.Y. Restricts Public-Employee Travel To North Carolina Over LGBT Law. NPR, https://www.npr.org/sec-tions/thetwo-way/2016/03/29/472268519/n-y-governor-bans-most-state-travel-to-north-carolina-over-lgbt-law.

Kindy, K. (2019, January 10). Tensions rise in federal prisons during shut-down as weary guards go without pay and work double shifts. The Washington Post, https://www.washingtonpost.com/national/tensions-rise-in-federal-prisons-during-shutdown-as-weary-guards-go-without-pay-and-work-double-shifts/2019/01/10/fc1042e8-136a-11e9-803c-4ef28312c8b9_story.html.

Microsoft Office (Microsoft Office 365) [Computer Software]. https://www.microsoft.com/en-us/microsoft-365.

Microsoft SharePoint (Microsoft Office 365) [Computer Software].

https://www.microsoft.com/en-us/microsoft-365/sharepoint/collaboration.

National Association of State Procurement Officers. (2022). https://www.naspo.org/.

Office of Attorney General. (2022). https://oag.ca.gov/ab1887.

Public Purchase. (2022). https://publicpurchase.com/gems/browse/home.

SBA Federal Contracting Assistance Programs. (2022). https://www.sba.gov/federal-contracting/contracting-assistance-programs.

USASpending.gov. (2022). https://www.usaspending.gov/explorer/object_class.

US Federal Reserve, Federal Reserve Bank of St. Louis. (2022, June 2). FRED Economic Data. Federal Reserve Bank of St. Louis. https://fred.stlouisfed.org/series/GDP#0

USGAO. A Snapshot of Government-wide Contracting for FY 2021 (Interactive Dashboard)

US General Services Administration, US Government System for Award Management. (2022, September 2). Contract Data Awards. US General Services Administration. https://sam.gov/api/prod/databank/v1/reports/static/download?fileName=Top_100_Contractors_Report_Fiscal_Year_2021&fileType=xlsx

US Goverment, System for Award Management. (2022, January 1). Opportunities. Sam.gov. https://sam.gov/reports/opp/standard

US Government, Government Accounting Office. (2022, August 25). A Snapshot of Government-wide Contracting for FY 2021.

Weintraub, D. (1992, August 30). Senate, Assembly OK Budget; Wilson Awaits Final Package. Los Angeles Times, https://www.latimes.com/archives/la-xpm-1992-08-30-mn-8555-story.html.

AUTHOR'S BIOGRAPHY

About the Author

Scott Johnson grew up in northern Minnesota and studied political science at Bemidji State University before enlisting in the Air Force for six years. After his service commitment, Scott worked as an IT manager for a sovereign wealth fund in the San Francisco Bay Area. Scott went on to form and operate several small technology and real estate businesses in California while making time to complete a bachelor of science degree. Eventually, he found himself in federal, state, and military contracting. Over the subsequent 15 years, Scott led several companies' sales efforts for professional services, software development, and data service contracts.

Scott returned to school a third time during the pandemic. He was accepted into a leading business school program, earning a Master of Business Administration (MBA) from the University of North Dakota. Scott now advises small and medium-sized businesses on government business development, proposal development, channel marketing, and sales capture strategies. Scott and his wife live in northern California and travel extensively with their RV throughout the year. They have one son, a daughter-in-law, and a grandson and are in their third decade of living with McNab Shepherds.

Scott's other books, services, and social media connections can be reached at https://www.granitebaywriter.com.

linkedin.com/in/scojohnson
twitter.com/LLCSSRJ
amazon.com/author/scojohnson

ACKNOWLEDGMENTS

Written by Scott Johnson

Edited by Scott Johnson

Cover Art by George Stevens, G Sharp Major Design LLC

Portrait Photo by Mikah Johnson, Photography by the Johnsons